The Right to Privacy

Bioethics & Culture Series
Edward J. Furton, General Editor

On Conscience
Joseph Cardinal Ratzinger
2007

The Right to Privacy
Janet E. Smith
2008

The National Catholic Bioethics Center was founded in 1972 to provide expert moral analysis and philosophical reflection in the fields of medicine, science, and technology. The NCBC seeks to promote and safeguard the dignity of the human person through research, education, consultation, and publishing. This mission, carried out for the sake of all people, is done with openness to the findings of science and with fidelity to the teachings of the Catholic Church. The NCBC includes among its key constituencies bishops and other clergy, health care workers and academics, those who shape law and public policy, and numerous individuals who seek clarity on critical health care issues affecting their families.

The National Catholic Bioethics Center
6399 Drexel Road
Philadelphia, PA 19151
www.ncbcenter.org

✠

The Right to Privacy

JANET E. SMITH

✠

With a Foreword by
Robert H. Bork

THE NATIONAL CATHOLIC BIOETHICS CENTER
Philadelphia

IGNATIUS PRESS   San Francisco

Published by
The National Catholic Bioethics Center
and Ignatius Press

Cover design by John Herreid

National Catholic Bioethics Center
ISBN: 978-0-935372-51-9

Ignatius Press
ISBN: 978-1-58617-259-6

Library of Congress control no. 2008018593

Library of Congress
Cataloging-in-Publication Data

Smith, Janet E., 1950-
  The right to privacy / Janet E. Smith, with a foreword by
Robert H. Bork.
     p. cm. -- (Bioethics & culture)
  Includes bibliographical references.
  ISBN 978-0-935372-51-9 (National Catholic Bioethics
Center) -- ISBN 978-1-58617-259-6 (Ignatius Press) 1.
Privacy, Right of--United States. 2. Human rights--United
States. 3. Ethics, Modern. I. Title.
  JC596.2.U5S63 2008
  323.44'80973--dc22
                                    2008018593

To Ralph McInerny

Contents

Foreword

The "right to privacy," ably deconstructed by Professor Janet E. Smith in this book, is but one of a series of phrases employed by the Supreme Court to justify the creation of rights not found in the Constitution by any traditional method of interpreting a legal document.

The list of such inventions is fairly well known, but among the more prominent is the warrantless attribution of substantive meaning to purely procedural guarantees. Thus, under the Due Process Clauses of the Fifth and Fourteenth Amendments ("No person ... shall be deprived of life, liberty, or property without due process of law") the Court has assumed the power to decide whether a law's substance is objectionable. In the first use of that illegitimate power, *Dred Scott v. Sandford* denied the right of the federal government to outlaw slavery in the territories.[1] Other cases required that statutes meet the standard of "ordered liberty."[2] One Justice suggested that a "right to dignity" sums up and vastly extends the particular guarantees of the Bill of Rights.[3] But perhaps the most grandiose and impenetrable verbal formula is that employed to create rights to abortion and homosexual sodomy: "At the heart of liberty [protected by the Constitution] is the right to define one's own concept of existence, of meaning, of the universe, and of the mystery of human life."[4] No one knows what that means except that laws regulating abortion and homosexual sodomy are now void. If the formula were taken seriously, which is manifestly impossible, most if not all laws regulating individual behavior would be unconstitutional. But perhaps it means only, as Justice Scalia said, that morals legislation is now constitutionally impermissible.[5]

It is to this genre of the indecipherable and the incoherent that the right to privacy belongs. No one can say, in advance of a Court ruling, what the right includes. Many acts done in private are nevertheless punishable by law, but we are not told what private behavior falls into the protected category and what does not, nor is there any hint of the criteria that define the area of guaranteed privacy.

What these judicial formulas have in common—from substantive due process to privacy (not to mention the right to your own concept of the mystery of human life)—is that no one who wrote or ratified the Constitution and the Bill of Rights contemplated the rights now asserted. There is no legislative history, no evidence of any original understanding or intent, to give a judge any guidance whatever. The judge who cites a right to privacy, for example, must make up its content. He must write the law without any authority outside his own preferences or views on appropriate public policy. That is not the rule of law; it is the essence of lawless judging.

It is hardly a surprise that the Court majority reflects the values, fads, and moods of the class—today, the intellectual class—that dominates the environment in which the judge operates. There is no need here to rehearse in detail what that means. Suffice it to say that for most of that class, the mood, in cultural matters, is primarily one favoring radical individual autonomy or moral relativism. The unkind would say "moral chaos." But that is not the main point here.

What is important for present purposes is that the Court, through the rights announced, including the right to privacy, has, intentionally or not (and I rather think not), set itself the impossible task of declaring, or at least following, principles that define when the state may coerce and when it may not. Any attempt to govern requires that the lawgiver strike a balance between freedom and coercion. The Bill of Rights does that by specifying particular areas of human autonomy that may not be invaded by government. The necessary additional rules are supplied by ordinary legislation or executive orders. But neither the Bill of Rights nor the additional rules are stated as universal principles; each deals with a specific topic. Any attempt to frame legislation or decrees with the generality of the right to privacy, for example, would be struck down as void for vagueness and, therefore, a denial of due process. No one could know in advance what obligations such legislation imposed upon them.

But the Court announces amorphous principles and quite specific results without explaining how the former lead to the latter, as in the mystery passage and homosexual sodomy. Unless one were to attribute the utmost bad faith to the Court's current majority, one must assume that the members of that majority have some notion, however vague, of a philosophy that determines the proper spheres of individual liberty and state coercion. That in turn assumes that such a philosophy is possible, though of course it is not. The problem, then, is not that the Justices who depart from and add to the specific provisions of Bill of Rights are incompetent as philosophers, though they obviously are; nor is the problem that no philosopher, however acute, has devised the necessary formula. The problem is that no such formula exists or can exist, as Lord Patrick Devlin demonstrated in his argument about the enforcement of morals by the criminal law.[6]

It follows that an activist judge, one who departs from the original understanding of specific guarantees or prohibitions, is condemned to wander from case to case with no guidance other than his own inclinations. The activist judge has a mood rather than a philosophy. In the case of the current Supreme Court majority, that mood bears a strong resemblance to political correctness. That in turn means the survival of *Roe v.*

Wade until more modest justices who refuse to accept blatant rewritings of the Constitution are appointed. The counterfeit right to privacy would be among the first rewritings jettisoned.

ROBERT H. BORK

Robert Bork was a judge on the U. S. Court of Appeals for the District of Columbia Circuit from 1982 to 1988. He is a Distinguished Senior Fellow at the Hudson Institute, the Tad and Dianne Taube Distinguished Visiting Fellow at the Hoover Institution, and a professor at Ave Maria School of Law.

1. *Dred Scott v. Sandford*, 60 U.S. 393 (1857).

2. "All that is meant is that due process contains within itself certain minimum standards which are 'of the very essence of a scheme of ordered liberty.'" *Adamson v. People of State of California*, 332 U.S. 46 (1947), at 65, Justice Reed, writing for the majority, citing *Palko v. Connecticut*, 302 U.S. 319 (1937), at 325.

3. See Justice William J. Brennan, Jr., "To the Text and Teaching Symposium," speech, Georgetown University, Washington, D.C., October 12, 1985.

4. *Planned Parenthood v. Casey*, 505 U.S. 833 (1992), at 851, Justice Kennedy, writing for the majority.

5. *Lawrence v. Texas*, 539 U.S. 558 (2003), at 2945, Justice Scalia, dissenting.

6. Lord Patrick Devlin, *The Enforcement of Morals* (London: Oxford University Press, 1965).

I
CULTURE WARS

Pope John Paul II's encyclical on life issues, *Evangelium vitae*, expresses support for the emergence of the concept of "fundamental rights" as a means of securing respect for human dignity:

> Various declarations of human rights and the many initiatives inspired by these declarations show that at the global level there is a growing moral sensitivity, more alert to acknowledging the value and dignity of every individual as a human being, without any distinction of race, nationality, religion, political opinion or social class.[1]

While lauding the benefits of the worldwide interest in human rights, *Evangelium vitae* notes that many actions previously recognized as crimes have now achieved the status of "rights." It claims that in spite of more frequent national and global proclamations defending fundamental rights, there has been a "tragic repudiation" of these rights in practice:

A new cultural climate is developing and taking hold, which gives crimes against life a new and—if possible—even more sinister character, giving rise to further grave concern: broad sectors of public opinion justify certain *crimes against life in the name of the rights of individual freedom*, and on this basis they claim not only exemption from punishment but even authorization by the State, so that these things can be done with total freedom and indeed with the free assistance of health-care systems. (n. 4, emphasis added)

Evangelium vitae endeavors to discover the roots of this erroneous view of freedom and finds them in skepticism, materialism, relativism, individualism, utilitarianism, hedonism, and ultimately in the loss of a "sense of God."[2]

The "right to privacy" is the logical offspring of these "isms." In this book we will see how it has been used by judges in the United States to remove legal sanctions against contraception, abortion, assisted suicide,[3] and homosexual acts. The presuppositions that drive these permissive legal decisions are in turn driven by the philosophies listed above. We will see how these philosophical outlooks, and the view of the human person that they imply, are incompatible with the Christian view of human dignity.

The dispute between those who argue that we have a right to contraception, abortion, assisted suicide, and homosexual activity and those who find these practices abhorrent is a dispute between those who disagree on the most fundamental principles for understanding reality and human life.[4] For example, concerning abortion and physician-assisted suicide, there are those, like Peter Singer, who believe that human beings (and even animals) who function at a higher cognitive level are more valuable than those who have not yet developed their abilities, who have reduced abilities, or who can no longer employ many of their distinctive human abilities.[5]

Then there are those who think that all who possess human nature, no matter at what stage of development, no matter what sex, race, or religion, and no matter how productive, thereby possess intrinsic worth.[6] Both sides speak of human rights, but the former contradicts in practice what it defends in theory. As *Evangelium vitae* states,

> We can find [the roots of this remarkable contradiction] in an overall assessment of a cultural and moral nature, beginning with the mentality which carries the concept of subjectivity to an extreme and even distorts it, and recognizes as a *subject of rights only the person who enjoys full or at least incipient autonomy and who emerges from a state of total dependence on others*. But how can we reconcile this approach with the exaltation of man as a being who is "not to be used"? The theory of human rights is based precisely on the affirmation that the human person, unlike animals and things, cannot be subjected to domination by others. (n. 19, emphasis added)

The debate is between those who think human beings are to be valued only when they function at a certain level and those who think that any being that is essentially human has full human rights.[7]

The dispute is also between those who believe the primary goal of government should be to protect radical individualism and others who think government should primarily seek to promote virtue and the common good. *Evangelium vitae* describes the first group:

> The more radical views go so far as to maintain that in a modern and pluralistic society people should be allowed complete freedom to dispose of their own lives as well as of the lives of the unborn: it is asserted that it is not the task of the law to choose between different moral opinions, and still less can the law claim to impose one particular opinion to the detriment of others. (n. 68)

Advocates of radical individualism think that freedom or autonomy is the greatest good and that the function of government is to ensure a wide range of choices of actions. They think that law, since it ensures public safety, is a necessary but unfortunate feature of life, because it regrettably curtails some human freedoms. They believe individual rights are more important than community life.

Promoters of the common good also value self-determination but believe that only those with virtue exercise the power of self-determination well. They understand virtue to be the good that government should promote above all others. Rather than promoting individual autonomy as the highest good, government should seek to build upon man's social nature and especially foster the virtue of justice, or fulfilling one's responsibilities to others. *Evangelium vitae* explains the Christian view of government:

> The real purpose of civil law is to guarantee an ordered social coexistence in true justice, so that all may "lead a quiet and peaceable life, godly and respectful in every way" (1 Tim 2:2). Precisely for this reason, civil law must ensure that all members of society enjoy respect for certain fundamental rights which innately belong to the person, rights which every positive law must recognize and guarantee. (n. 71)

The most important responsibilities of the state are to protect the innocent from harm, to promote a culture in which children are raised to become responsible adults, and in which responsible adults can live out their lives in pursuit of truth and goodness. According to this view, law is one of man's greatest achievements, because it permits man to shape a world in which individuals in a community have abundant opportunity to pursue what is good and fulfilling to their natures.[8]

People on one side of the cultural war think it is impossible to know the truth about ultimate matters. Skeptics and historicists think that it is not possible to transcend our own subjectively generated or culturally determined readings of reality. *Evangelium vitae* describes this view:

> If it is believed that an objective truth shared by all is de facto unattainable, then respect for the freedom of the citizens—who in a

> democratic system are considered the true rulers—would require that on the legislative level the autonomy of individual consciences be acknowledged. Consequently, when establishing those norms which are absolutely necessary for social coexistence, the only determining factor should be the will of the majority, whatever this may be. (n. 69)

Those on the other side think it is impossible to operate without a foundation of truth. They understand that there is an objective order to the world that needs to be respected, and that the failure to recognize objective truth leads to a tyranny of opinion and whim. There is a powerful description of this claim also in *Evangelium vitae*:

> Freedom negates and destroys itself, and becomes a factor leading to the destruction of others, when it no longer recognizes and respects its essential link with the truth. When freedom, out of a desire to emancipate itself *from all forms of tradition and authority*, shuts out even *the most obvious evidence of an objective and universal truth*, which is the foundation of personal and social life, then the person ends up by no longer taking as the sole and indisputable point of reference for his own choices the truth about good and evil, but only his *subjective and changeable opinion* or, indeed, his *selfish interest and whim*. (n. 19, emphasis added)

Thus, there is now a war within our culture between those who think human freedom requires that the law recognize "rights" to such actions as abortion and assisted suicide, and others who think the objective truths of reality, and especially human dignity, require that the law protect those who are the most vulnerable, including the unborn and the dying.

In sum, the conflict is between those who think that moral values are relative and that the subjective opinions of the individual should govern his or her choices, and those who think there are some moral absolutes and that truth and concern for the common good should govern our choices.

As one can see, radical philosophical differences are the backdrop of the cultural war in which we find ourselves—a cultural war that has grown into confrontations among members of the same churches and communities, among citizens of the same nations, and among nations. There are many ways to illustrate the various manifestations of the cultural war; for instance, the debate is being played out on a global level in the discussions at the United Nations on reproductive rights. One side seeks to ensure that even very young people in all countries have abundant access to contraceptives, sterilization, and abortion; the other side finds such policies an assault on the family.[9] That assault does not stop with "reproductive rights" but quite inevitably expands to include pressure to permit access to assisted suicide and euthanasia and the legal recognition of same-sex unions. There is some logic to these connections, one that the courts' repeated appeal to the right to privacy makes explicit.

In reviewing how key court decisions display these connections, this book confirms the analysis of *Evangelium vitae* that one of the foundations of the Culture of Death is a "mentality which carries the concept of subjectivity to an extreme and even distorts it" (n. 19). We will see that the elevation of the right to privacy to a near absolute status stems from a sharp break with "all forms of tradition and authority" and that it fosters a selfish individualism. It will become clear that the "right to privacy" has undergone several transformations to emerge as a commitment to radical autonomy—that is, to an enshrinement of the freedom to make one's own decisions using a subjective reading of reality and one's individual perception of what are ultimate goods.[10] And, more briefly, we will see that the lifestyles enabled by these new "rights" to previously illegal actions have led to demands for ever greater opportunities to exercise autonomous decision making over areas traditionally subject to legislative proscriptions and government regulations. For example, the "right to privacy" cases reviewed in the following chapters have paved the way for the legal recognition of homosexual acts as constitutionally protected in *Lawrence v. Texas*.[11]

One caveat: The intent here is not to propose kinds of legislation that could be written against such actions as contraception, abortion, assisted suicide, or homosexual behavior. Indeed, simply to determine that an action is immoral and that it harms society or individuals is not sufficient to establish that it should be the object of legislation. Laws that are possible and appropriate concerning an action are determined not only by their moral status and their possible consequences for a culture, but also by other factors, such as the possibility of achieving consensus and the enforceability of such laws in a given time and place. For instance, it has long been thought that some vices are simply so pervasive and so personal that they are beyond the reach of law (e.g., overeating or laziness). Certainly, self-determination is of great value, and any curtailment of human freedom must not be considered a negligible factor. Indeed, since virtue is fostered by voluntary rather than coerced actions, fostering virtue through nonlegislative means is always preferable.

Let us also note that the legality of an action should not be construed to mean that legislators are expressing agnosticism about the morality of the action. John Stuart Mill, a great advocate of liberty, had no difficulty pronouncing many actions morally wrong, but argued that, even so, the state should permit them for many of the reasons stated above. (He also approved laws over areas that we generally think are now beyond the reach of law; for example, he did not object to laws requiring those seeking to get married to be able to demonstrate financial stability.[12]) In these skeptical and relativistic times, however, the absence of laws against actions is often understood to mean that we have no means to determine the morality of the action or that the action is not sufficiently harmful to warrant legal sanction.

This book is not the place to explain why contraception, abortion, assisted suicide, and homosexual acts are immoral; suffice it to say that I accept the evaluation provided by the Catholic Church about these actions. Nor, as stated, will I propose legislation. Rather, my intention is simply to show that the right to privacy has been used to legitimize a radical view of personal autonomy over areas that have been traditionally thought to be within the proper province of law, and to show that this is one reason why actions that were at one time considered abominable crimes are now considered inalienable rights.

II

A Distorted Understanding of Rights

As noted in Chapter 1, *Evangelium vitae* claims that a distorted understanding of rights has fueled the Culture of Death; indeed, it claims that what are properly crimes have been converted into rights:

> A problem ... exists at the cultural, social and political level, where it reveals its more sinister and disturbing aspect in the tendency, ever more widely shared, to interpret ... crimes against life as legitimate expressions of individual freedom, to be acknowledged and protected as actual rights.

> In this way, and with tragic consequences, a long historical process is reaching a turning-point. The process which once led to discovering the idea of "human rights"—rights inherent in every person and prior to any Constitution and State legislation—is today marked by a surprising contradiction. Precisely in an age when the inviolable rights of the person are solemnly

> proclaimed and the value of life is publicly affirmed, the very right to life is being denied or trampled upon, especially at the more significant moments of existence: the moment of birth and the moment of death. (n. 18, emphasis added)

Pope John Paul II considers laws that attack life to be a

> direct threat to the entire culture of human rights ... a threat capable, in the end, of jeopardizing the very meaning of democratic coexistence: rather than societies of "people living together," our cities risk becoming societies of people who are rejected, marginalized, uprooted and oppressed. (n.18)

In the end, he maintains that unless advocacy for fundamental rights includes the right to life, "affirmation of the rights of individuals and peoples made in distinguished international assemblies is a merely futile exercise of rhetoric" (n.18).

In recent decades, the Catholic Church has increasingly expressed its moral and political teaching in terms of "rights language."[1] Clearly, the above passages from *Evangelium vitae* welcome universal recognition of rights in service of human dignity, but it also acknowledges the danger of a reckless assertion of rights. Before addressing the right to privacy more specifically, I will make some general remarks about the predominance of "rights language" in our political and moral discourse. Here I follow to a great extent the work of Mary Ann Glendon, whose work *Rights Talk: The Impoverishment of Political Discourse* is of immense value for those seeking to understand the limits that rights language places upon our ability to discuss legal and moral matters.

Glendon establishes that rights language is the coin of the day as far as moral discourse is concerned: that is, if one tries to make a case for morality in the modern age, it is nearly impossible to do so without recourse to rights language. Whenever we want to speak of an action as morally wrong, we generally attempt to find some "right" that has been violated; when we wish to stake a claim to some good, we assert that we have a right to it. We have a very difficult time employing other language traditionally associated with morality and political life, language that speaks of virtue and vice, good and evil, duties and obligations.[2]

Rights language has considerable benefits: it carries with it a salutary dimension that to some extent serves to combat the relativism of modern times. Reference to fundamental inalienable rights suggests that there is a universal and absolute set of moral demands, true at all times and places. International codes of human rights have promise for extending justice and respect for human dignity throughout the world. Indeed, rights language, with its universalizing tendency, is difficult to defend without reference to truth that transcends time and culture. Indeed, Justice William Douglas in *Griswold v. Connecticut*, the court case that struck down laws against contraception, stated that the right to privacy is "older than the Bill of Rights," a phrase which suggests a transcendent status to the right.[3]

It is ironic that the same courts that deny the existence of *objective, universal* moral norms have advanced the right to privacy as a *fundamental, universal* right. They also selectively allow appeal to God as a source of rights. For instance, while the courts refuse to allow appeals to revelation to support the claim of the unborn's humanity, they assert that the liberties they choose to advance are God-given. Justice Paul Stevens, one of the most ardent proponents of the "right to privacy," explicitly connected legal attempts to protect liberty with a Creator, the source of transcendent laws. In explaining why "liberty interests" exist despite the fact that they appear neither in the Constitution nor in state law, he refers to God as a source of that liberty:

> [The law] is not the source of liberty, and surely not the exclusive source. ... I had thought it self-evident that all men were endowed by their Creator with liberty as one of the cardinal unalienable rights. It is that basic freedom which the Due Process Clause protects, rather than the particular rights or privileges conferred by specific laws or regulations.[4]

This appeal to a "self-evident" truth, to "inalienable rights" and "basic freedom," looks suspiciously like the assertion of universal objective truths. And is there not an appeal to religion in reference to "the Creator"? Why does Stevens use this language? Perhaps he senses that rights untethered to some transcendent reality become man-made, shifting and arbitrary: he does not want the "right to privacy" to be his private invention, but to be something required by objective reality. It is important to note that advocates of privacy utilize the very language that they reject when it is used to defend the unborn.[5]

Evangelium vitae detects another irony. It notes that the elevation of the individual freedom of some has led to the violation of the freedom of others, and speaks of "two diametrically opposed tendencies":

> On the one hand, individuals claim for themselves in the moral sphere the most complete freedom of choice and demand that the State should not adopt or impose any ethical position but limit itself to guaranteeing maximum space for the freedom of each individual, with the sole limitation of not infringing on the freedom and rights of any other citizen. On the other hand, it is held that, in the exercise of public and professional duties, respect for other people's freedom of choice requires that each one should set aside his or her own convictions in order to satisfy every demand of the citizens which is recognized and guaranteed by law; in carrying out one's duties the only moral criterion should be what is laid down by the law itself. Individual responsibility is thus turned over to the civil law, with a renouncing of personal conscience, at least in the public sphere. (n. 69)

A good example of a law that protects the choices of some but violates the consciences of others is Canadian bill 250C, which prohibits public speech against homosexuality. So, too, are laws in the United States that create "buffer zones" at abortion clinics to separate protestors from abortion clinic clientele.[6] The "right to privacy" and the actions it justifies have become rights that trump other fundamental rights, even such revered rights as freedom of speech.

Another irony is that, in spite of the tendency of rights to be hailed as universal and absolute, rights language is increasingly employed in the service of relativism and subjectivism. It is invoked to expand access to practices, such as abortion, suicide, and homosexual acts, that historically have been considered immoral by a wide range of nations, cultures, religions, and philosophies.[7]

A serious problem with rights language is that it is difficult to establish what a right is and what the foundation is for any given right. Some rights, often called "negative rights," describe what is known as a "zone of noninterference." To say, for instance, that one has a "right to life" or a "right to privacy" means that there is some realm of human existence that should remain free from attack or intrusion by others. Other rights, known as "positive" rights, make claims on a person or institution to provide something to another. For instance, children are said to have a right to food, shelter, clothing, and education from their parents. It is not always clear whether a right is negative or positive or, in the case of positive rights, who has the obligation or duty to supply the need. For instance, it is not immediately clear whether rights to a job or to health care are negative or positive and, if positive, who has the obligation to provide jobs and health care. Furthermore, some rights, such as the right not to be raped, are absolute, whereas other rights can be overridden, such as the right to property. Some rights are fundamental, such as the right to a just wage, but what exact payment is required for a just wage is relative to a given time and place.

As our preliminary discussion has disclosed, a key question has already arisen: What or who is the source of rights? Does the state confer rights upon us? Are they God-given? One could ask these questions differently: Are rights simply a legal invention or are there fundamental human rights? Are they inherent in us because of our humanity or personhood? Furthermore, what is the good that they serve? Liberty? Dignity? A peaceful society? And, indeed, how do we determine what our rights are? What grounds a right to freedom of speech? A right to the free practice of religion? A right to abortion? Can reason disclose to us what our rights are? Are they self-evident or divinely revealed, or just the product of the accumulated wisdom of society? And finally, are there limits to these rights? Are there occasions when we should voluntarily sacrifice them for the sake of other goods? Are there occasions when we should be compelled to do so? Do certain behaviors or even beliefs merit the forfeiture of these rights? Are there any rights that can never be denied?

Our failure as a culture to find answers to these questions has led to what Glendon calls a proliferation of rights—again, we tend to assert a "right" to anything which we desire. At one time in Canada there was a group of women lobbying for wages for housewives as a right. Some states and countries have extended the right to marriage to homosexuals. Glendon observes that we seem to have abandoned all other terminology for expressing moral demands and outrage, for making claims to what we think is rightly ours. The following passage from Glendon's book articulates some of the problems with "rights talk":

> Our rights talk, in its absoluteness, promotes unrealistic expectations, heightens social conflict, and inhibits dialogue that might lead toward consensus, accommodation, or at least the discovery of common ground. In its silence concerning responsibilities, it seems to condone acceptance of the benefits of living in a democratic social welfare state, without accepting the corresponding personal and civic obligations. In its relentless individualism, it fosters a climate that is inhospitable to society's losers, and that systematically disadvantages caretakers and dependents, young and old. In its neglect of civic society, it undermines the principle seedbeds of civic and personal virtue.[8]

Note Glendon's claim that rights talk eclipses all talk of responsibility. She observes that young people are able to recite a litany of the rights that are secured by a free society but are not able to list what obligations and responsibilities members of a free society might have. She maintains that rights talk reduces each of us to an autonomous bundle of rights that is independent of relationships and of the community. We become so concerned with securing our own rights that we exhibit little interest in the well-being of others. In fact, others are seen as potential rivals for the goods to which we believe we have rights.

The modern emphasis on our rights as individuals to whatever we think is necessary to our subjective understanding of what is good leads us to discount our obligations to help others achieve what is good for them. The fact that human beings are social animals often seems to have been lost as a fundamental principle in our moral discourse and political decision making. And by social here, I mean to assert that our well-being necessitates that our lives be embedded in a vastly complicated net of relationships with our parents, grandparents, and siblings; our neighbors and friends and fellow citizens; shop owners, physicians, mechanics—indeed, in relationships with perfect strangers and all members of the human community, dead, alive, and yet to be born. These relationships necessarily entail a host of duties and obligations, relationships that are not well served by rights language. For instance, to speak of a child's right to receive food, shelter, and love from his or her parents, and to speak of parents honoring their children's rights when they fulfill their children's needs, surely falsifies the parent–child relationship. The rights language that undergirds abortion also falsifies the relationship between mother and child in the womb, and one of the most natural loving relationships becomes characterized as a relationship involving competing rights—the right to choose versus the right to life.[9]

III

THE RIGHT TO PRIVACY

All those who have written on the right to privacy agree that it has not been a well-defined concept. For instance, abortion advocate Judith Jarvis Thompson observes, "Perhaps the most striking thing about the right to privacy is that nobody seems to have any very clear idea what it is."[1] Yet there seems to be some consensus that there are areas of life that can properly be deemed private and, in fact, are so private that they should not be subject to public scrutiny or state regulation. Cultural anthropologists believe they have found a universal need and respect for privacy, but find a wide diversity in cultures for what areas of life this includes.[2] Within cultures, privacy expectations and needs may vary. In our culture, such activities as urinating, having sexual intercourse, and writing in personal journals have been considered private. The proliferation of "reality" television and webcasts that capture every moment of individuals' lives indicates that Americans are perhaps not quite so attached to privacy as they might suppose. The "privacy" they do value is the "right" to do whatever they like—which includes transgressing the boundaries of what is properly private!

The modern age that puts such a premium on individualism, relativism, and skepticism finds the right to privacy to be a nearly self-evident right; but, again, the writers of the Constitution and Bill of Rights did not explicitly regard it as in need of special protection, and it may even have been unknown to them.[3] It is a right that has progressively taken over the right to property, a right upon which many other rights have traditionally depended, including the nascent right to privacy. Glendon's book is a valuable resource here as well. She traces, via John Locke and his disciples, how the right to property came to be considered an almost absolute right, making the right to private property a symbol and even foundation for all other rights. Glendon explains how Locke built upon the idea that the body is our private property and anything invested in the work of our bodies is ours as well.[4] The purpose of government, in Locke's view, was to protect private property.

Whereas Locke was primarily interested in promoting the right to private property as a way of diminishing the divine right of kings, William Blackstone, whose thought provided the foundation of American views on property rights, went beyond Locke in elevating the individual to a tyrant or despot over his own property, and held that property rights are "absolute, individual, and exclusive."[5] Although property rights have not, in fact, been inviolate in American law, Glendon argues that the rhetoric surrounding the right to property has often elevated it to an absolute status.[6]

Glendon maintains that the tendency to speak of the right to property as absolute has extended to the right to privacy:[7]

> Much of the attention the Supreme Court once lavished on a broad concept of property ... it now devotes to certain personal liberties that it has designated as "fundamental." Remarkably, the property paradigm, including the old language of absoluteness, broods over this developing jurisprudence of personal rights. The new right of privacy, like the old right of property, has been imagined by the Court and lawyers generally as marking off a protected sphere surrounding the individual.[8]

The right to privacy was, as Glendon states, "quite literally pulled from the hat of property."[9]

The right to privacy was first brought to the attention of the American legal community in an article that addressed the illegality of publicizing thoughts expressed in private or actions that are inherently private.[10] In 1890, Samuel D. Warren and Louis D. Brandeis wrote an article titled "The Right to Privacy,"[11] which was not about constitutional law but about private tort remedy. Their concern was to protect individuals from the intrusiveness of photography and the press, from publicizing private communications without one's consent. They found a basis for the right to privacy in the right to property: our words and thoughts are like our property and need to be protected, but they maintained that the right to privacy should be identified as its own separate right.

Warren and Brandeis define the right to privacy most succinctly as the "right to be let alone":

> [Our] considerations lead to the conclusion that the protection afforded to thoughts, sentiments, and emotions, expressed through the medium of writing or of the arts, so far as it consists in preventing publication, is merely an instance of the enforcement of the more general right of the individual to be let alone. It is like the right not to be assaulted or beaten, the right not to be imprisoned, the right not to be maliciously prosecuted, the right not to be defamed. In each of these rights, as indeed in all other rights recognized by the law, there inheres the quality of being owned or possessed—and (as that is the distinguishing attribute of property) there may be some propriety in speaking of those rights as property. But, obviously, they bear little resemblance to what is ordinarily comprehended under that term. The principle which protects personal writings and all other personal productions, not against theft and physical appropriation, but against publication in any form, is in reality not the principle of private property, but that of an inviolate personality.[12]

As the above passage maintains, the right to privacy is understood here as the right to have one's thoughts not published against one's will—in its original setting it had nothing to do with radical autonomy. Indeed, nothing in Warren and Brandeis's article suggests that the right to privacy involves anything like the right to abortion or the right to define reality as one would like. In fact, most philosophical inquiry and legal scholarship focus primarily upon privacy as a right that protects one's nonmaterial property and reputation; little of it has to do with right to privacy as connected with autonomous choices.[13]

For all the influence that Warren and Brandeis's article has had, they failed to provide a precise definition of privacy beyond the "right to be let alone." Edward Bloustein notes that they were more successful in identifying what they did not mean by the "right to privacy" than in articulating what they did mean.[14] Those who comment on Warren and Brandeis and on cases that invoke the right to privacy find very different meanings for it.[15] I do not intend here to do an exhaustive review of the literature or analysis of the concept. For our purposes it may be sufficient to note that the "right to privacy" has come to be understood as encompassing at least the following three general categories:

1. The right not to have information about one's self made public without one's consent.[16] For instance, tapping phone lines is regulated by law.

2. The right not to have certain private spaces, such as the body or the home, subject to intrusion.[17] For instance, one's home cannot be subject to search and seizure without due cause.

3. The right to self-determination in making decisions about one's life.[18] For instance, the state may not designate whom one is to marry.

The "right to privacy" has clearly undergone a striking metamorphosis. In the court cases that are of interest here, the right to privacy has generally been used in reference to a "private place" or to a choice that should be "autonomous," matters far removed from not publicizing private information. For instance, as we will see, contraception was legalized largely with reference to the sanctity of a place (the bedroom) and the value of self-determination, which would leave it to couples to determine when to reproduce. The establishment of abortion as a constitutionally protected action was based on an understanding of the inviolateness of the body and the right of a woman to exercise self-determination over her child-bearing practices. Arguments that defend assisted suicide often have some reference to "place" or at least ownership—one's body or one's life is understood to be one's own, but talk of the "liberty to determine the time and manner of one's death" suggests powerful concerns with autonomy.[19] As we will see, a right that embraces not only the right to keep one's diary private but the right to ask for medical assistance in killing oneself is an elastic right indeed.

In many of its applications the right to privacy has not been considered absolute, that is, it has been subject to being "trumped" by state interest to protect other rights and goods. If it can be shown that to protect the common good the state must tap a phone line, it will do so. If there is reasonable cause to suspect that criminal activity is being or has been conducted in a private space, intrusion is permitted; for instance, the state allows schools to require mandatory drug testing of students (which can require observed urination) and will provide search warrants for privately owned property. The state has had a great deal of say over whom one can marry: it has excluded some categories of individuals as marriage partners. Parents cannot, for instance, marry their own children. Yet, although the law in many respects does not treat the "right to privacy" as inviolate, when it comes to the questions of abortion and homosexual behavior, attempts to restrict these practices out of concern for the common good are met with fierce resistance.

The ultimate philosophical justifications for the above categories of privacy remain largely unarticulated. Why is it wrong to make some information about individuals public? Why should certain spaces be inviolate? Why would it be wrong for the state to try to regulate certain human actions? To answer these questions sufficiently would require a full-blown anthropology and eventually a complete theory of the nature and purpose of the state as well—and that is surely beyond our scope here. But some brief attempt at an answer must be made.

Ultimately, the claims for a right to privacy seem rooted in the distinctive nature of mankind. Dominant strains of Western philosophy have understood human beings to be unique among all other creatures that inhabit this earth. They are rational and free animals; they differ from all other animals because their actions are not simply the product of innate natural inclinations. They can freely choose to act upon certain desires in the light of a cognitive understanding of what is good and what is evil. Unlike all other creatures, they are free to assess the moral dimensions of thoughts, desires, and actions—the dimensions of actions that threaten harm to others and to self. The dominant strains of Western philosophy that defend this view of the human person argue that man's freedom is best explained by the fact that he has a spiritual element, a soul, that is not confined by the restraints of matter.

Furthermore, the respect given to human freedom historically has stemmed from the principle that nature is good and must be respected. Since human beings are naturally free, we believe we must respect that freedom; human beings live most fully when they are free to make choices about matters that affect their lives, especially those that are most intimate.

It is ironic in the extreme that some of those who are the fiercest advocates of radical autonomy often claim that there are no spiritual realities and see no reason to "respect" nature. They believe all is matter, that matter is determined, and that anything material can be manipulated in any way that advances some good or preference.[20] Making a case for human freedom and finding a reason to respect human freedom within those parameters are difficult, if not impossible.

So "privacy concerns" in their many manifestations have been highly valued as connected to the very meaning of personhood: control of our thoughts, control of many features of life within the home, control over life choices such as marriage, childbearing, careers, and how to dispose of one's time and property have been thought to be portions of life not properly subject to state control, especially in societies that respect human freedom.

There are many reasons why human beings may need to keep some of their thoughts and actions private.[21] For instance, it can be argued that persons need a private realm in order to develop the riches of their personhood; to develop thoughts and make choices that shape their character; to be free not to share some of those thoughts; and to be free to perform some of their actions apart from the gaze of the impersonal public. It may be that making some thoughts and actions public may threaten our freedom to shape and reshape ourselves. Intimacy seems necessary to human fulfillment—we cannot develop our social natures without intimacy, and intimacy by its very nature means that we share with only a few what we do not share with others. Intimacy allows us to entrust vulnerabilities—dreams, hopes, and fears—to those who will not take advantage of us.

Moreover, the principle of subsidiarity may support a need for privacy: those who are "closest" to a situation, and who have the most invested in it, should be the ones making the decision. Mature individuals are usually best able to select friends, careers, and spouses for themselves, and adults should even be permitted to choose badly so long as the damage done to others and themselves is not great.

Certainly, there are realms of life that generally should not be subject to state regulation, and this is the "private" realm.

In spite of the high regard for privacy and its necessity in some realms for full human development, no one denies that there are necessary limitations on the exercise of human freedom. This necessity also flows from the nature of the human being: we are not only rational and free, we also are social animals—that is, we must live in groups in order to survive and to thrive. Thus, our freedom to pursue a certain line of action must occasionally, if not often, be curtailed, since some of our choices affect the well-being of others and may even be so destructive to ourselves that we need protection from ourselves. Americans, purported to be fierce advocates of autonomy and privacy, have become accustomed to regulations that could be seen as quite remarkable violations of autonomy and privacy, such as the mandatory use of seat belts and bike helmets and the strict regulation of various medical treatments.

In spite of legal precedence for limiting exercise of the right to privacy, to succeed in designating an activity private nonetheless carries considerable weight against any effort at regulation. That is, once contraception and abortion were justified as protected by the right to privacy, the possibility of placing any legal restrictions on them became extremely difficult. Let us now trace how the right to privacy was used to make such actions legal.

IV

GRISWOLD AND CONTRACEPTION

The centrality of the "right to privacy" to our public reasoning about moral matters emerged most vividly in the effort to overturn laws that prohibited the sale, counsel, and use of contraception. Such laws seem archaic and repressive to the contemporary mind; surely only tyrants or prudes could countenance them—or some institution as archaic as the Catholic Church. The opposition to contraception as a serious moral evil is often thought to be exclusively Catholic. Yet in 1873, Anthony Comstock, a Protestant, persuaded a largely Protestant Congress to pass the "Comstock Law," which forbade the mailing of any promotional material about contraception or contraceptives; this law passed because legislators understood the use of contraceptives to be a source of vice—they were something a man would use with a mistress or prostitute, not his spouse.[1] Few realize that all Christian churches,[2] Orthodox Judaism, and such renowned Hindus as Gandhi have also been opposed to contraceptives. Anglicans at the 1930 Lambeth conference were the first Protestants to approve the use of contraception within marriage for serious reasons.

The teaching against contraception was virtually unchallenged in the Catholic Church until the invention of the birth control pill.[3] Yet since the publication of *Humanae vitae* in 1968, this teaching has been rejected by leading theologians, rarely and weakly taught by bishops, and widely disregarded in practice.[4] Certainly most mainline Protestant churches currently accept contraception, although there is a growing rejection of contraception among Evangelicals for many of the same reasons that the Catholic Church opposes it:[5] it is a rejection of the procreative power of the sexual act; it prevents spouses from giving of themselves completely within marriage; and it leads to considerable social chaos by contributing to the incidence of promiscuity, unwed pregnancy, abortion, single parenthood, and divorce. [6]

The story of the battle to make the counsel and use of contraceptives legal in the state of Connecticut displays the perseverance of many individuals, particularly the directors and legal counsel of Planned Parenthood. Those who worked for over forty years to overturn the laws of Connecticut and Massachusetts (supported by the presidents of Amherst, Brown, Dartmouth, and Yale when originally passed) had multiple strategies. After trying to repeal the laws in the legislatures several times and being repeatedly thwarted, they decided that getting the courts to judge the laws to be unconstitutional was their best hope. As Russell Hittinger states, "Every time that liberalization [of laws against contraception], much less repeal, came before the people in the form of referenda or legislative bills, the votes were not even close."[7] The imperial Court, the court that has run roughshod over laws passed through the democratic process, began long before *Roe v. Wade*, the case that overturned the laws against abortion in every state of the union.

It was with the development of the birth control pill and its widespread use in the 1960s that legal challenges against laws forbidding the counsel and use of contraceptives succeeded.[8] *Griswold v. Connecticut* (1965) struck down laws prohibiting the use, distribution, and counseling of contraceptives.[9] These were laws that had not, in fact, been enforced against married couples or vendors but were perceived as a threat to the activities of Planned Parenthood, which was, at that time, distributing contraceptives.

The basis for striking down these provisions is extremely important. As I have noted, the invocation of the right to privacy, a right that is not mentioned explicitly in the Constitution or the Bill of Rights and that historically had been confined to making private matters public, was key.

As David Garrow portrays in his book *Liberty and Sexuality: The Right to Privacy and the Making of* Roe v. Wade, the justices of the Supreme Court were not of one mind on what basis they could rightly overturn the law. After all, the laws had been duly legislated by the state legislatures, which repeatedly resisted efforts of repeal, and had been upheld by the state courts and courts of appeal.[10] The justices toyed with locating a constitutional right to use contraceptives in several of the amendments to the Constitution: it was argued that contraception violates the First Amendment because doctors have freedom of speech, patients have freedom of information, and spouses have freedom of association; it violates the Fourth and Fifth Amendments because man has a right to the sanctity of his own home; it violates the Ninth Amendment because people have more rights than those explicitly protected by the Constitution; and it violates the Fourteenth because the rich should not have access to contraception while the poor do not. In the end the Court found the "right to privacy" "in the penumbra of specific guarantees of the Bill of Rights" and not in any specific amendment, although it has been increasingly identified with the "substantive due process clause" of the Fourteenth Amendment.[11]

Griswold's precise understanding of the right to privacy is not clear. It did express horror at the thought of the law invading the bedroom:[12]

> Such a law cannot stand in light of the familiar principle, so often applied by this Court, that a "governmental purpose to control or prevent activities constitutionally subject to state regulation may not be achieved by means which sweep unnecessarily broadly and thereby invade the area of protected freedoms." Would we allow the police to search the sacred precincts

> of marital bedrooms for telltale signs of
> the use of contraceptives? The very idea is
> repulsive to the notions of privacy surround-
> ing the marriage relationship. ... We deal
> with a right of privacy older than the Bill
> of Rights—older than our political parties,
> older than our school system.[13]

Talk here of the "sacred precincts" of the bedroom seems a bit hyperbolic, although surely there is some truth to the claim that most of what married couples do in the bedroom should be beyond the reach of the law. If not hyperbolic, the phrase seems imprecise, since the law does forbid marital rape, incest, and sexual intercourse with children even when it happens in the bedroom. Obviously, the bedroom is not beyond the prov-ince of law. Thus, the Court cannot mean that the bedroom is an absolute sanctuary. Clearly, it is not the "space" that so deserves protection but a certain activity that generally takes place in a bedroom. Indeed, at the time of *Griswold*, several of the justices remained adamant that, except for marital intercourse, sexual activity occurring in the bedroom was subject to regulation by the state. *Bowers v. Hardwick* (1986),[14] later to be overturned by *Lawrence v. Texas* (2003),[15] upheld laws against homosexual intercourse, that, in the instance considered by the Court, had taken place in the bedroom. It should be noted that in their concurring statement in *Griswold*, Justices Goldberg, Douglas, and Brennan acknowledged the interest of the state in forbidding fornication, adultery, homosexuality, and other sexual misconduct. Their statement maintains that "the State of Connecticut does have statutes, the constitutionality of which is beyond doubt, which prohibit adultery and fornication" and "finally, it should be said of the Court's holding today that it in no way interferes with a State's proper regulation of sexual promiscuity or misconduct."[16]

In 1972, in *Eisenstadt v. Baird*, the right to privacy was found to extend to allow the unmarried access to contraception, not on the basis of the sanctity of the bedroom but on the basis of the right of individuals to determine whether to bear or beget a child:

> If under *Griswold* the distribution of contraceptives to married persons cannot be prohibited, a ban on distribution to unmarried persons would be equally impermissible. It is true that in *Griswold* the right of privacy in question inhered in the marital relationship. Yet the marital couple is not an independent entity with a mind and heart of its own, but an association of two individuals each with a separate intellectual and emotional makeup. *If the right of privacy means anything*, it is the right of the individual, married or single, to be free from unwarranted governmental intrusion into matters so fundamentally affecting a person as the decision whether to bear or beget a child. [17]

The phrase "if the right to privacy means anything" is strong language; it suggests that "reproductive rights" are at the very heart of the right to privacy and not just a justifiable extension of the right. Whereas *Griswold* spoke of a "marital right to privacy," *Eisenstadt* holds that "reproductive rights" belong to the single person as much as to the married couple. Whereas *Griswold* spoke of the "sacred precincts of the bedroom," *Eisenstadt* speaks of the "decision whether to bear or beget a child."[18] The inclusion of the term "to bear a child" ups the ante considerably; the choice to beget a child involves the decision whether or not to engage in intercourse, whereas the decision to bear a child has life and death implications for the embryo or fetus and thus is not in the same category as "begetting."

Again, my purpose here is not so much to determine the behavior over which the state has proper jurisdiction, but to analyze the reasoning that has invoked the right to privacy to establish contraception and abortion as rights and that may soon use it to classify assisted suicide and same-sex marriages as rights. In *Eisenstadt* we see some early shifting of the sands: it is not the privacy of the bedroom or the privacy of the marital act that defines the zone of noninterference; rather, the right to privacy is now construed as individuals being free to decide whether or not to beget or bear a child.

Whereas Warren and Brandeis had spoken of a right to privacy that entitles an individual "to decide whether that which is his shall be given to the public," the courts increasingly speak of the "right to privacy" in conjunction with the right to autonomy and to liberty and a right to a zone of private conduct with which the law cannot interfere. Indeed, in *Griswold*, the "right to privacy" was elevated to a fundamental and basic right on the order of something guaranteed by natural law (or God, or nature?).[19] We find there the statement, "We deal with a right of privacy older than the Bill of Rights—older than our political parties, older than our school system."[20] Justice Black (joined by Stewart) in his dissent in *Griswold* complained precisely about this elevation and about the usurpation by the Court of legislative prerogatives:

> Observing that "the right of privacy . . . presses for recognition here," today this Court, which I did not understand to have power to sit as a court of common law, now appears to be exalting a phrase which Warren and Brandeis used in discussing grounds for tort relief, to the level of a constitutional rule which prevents state legislatures from passing any law deemed by this Court to interfere with "privacy."[21]

Black protested against the idea that the right to privacy is absolute: "I like my privacy as well as the next one, but I am nevertheless compelled to admit that government has a right to invade it unless prohibited by some specific constitutional provision."[22]

Justice Black also found a dangerous elasticity to the notion of the right to privacy and argued that the Court could use the concept to declare unconstitutional any legislation they did not like:

> One of the most effective ways of diluting or expanding a constitutionally guaranteed right is to substitute for the crucial word or words of a constitutional guarantee another

word or words, more or less flexible and more or less restricted in meaning. This fact is well illustrated by the use of the term "right of privacy" as a comprehensive substitute for the Fourth Amendment's guarantee against "unreasonable searches and seizures." "Privacy" is a broad, abstract and ambiguous concept which can easily be shrunken in meaning but which can also, on the other hand, easily be interpreted as a constitutional ban against many things other than searches and seizures.[23]

And further:

I discuss the due process and Ninth Amendment arguments together because on analysis they turn out to be the same thing—merely using different words to claim for this Court and the federal judiciary power to invalidate any legislative act which the judges find irrational, unreasonable, or offensive.[24]

Now let us turn to a set of court cases that utilize the "right to privacy" as a kind of wild card in decisions dealing with moral issues, issues about which the court seems to have a different moral evaluation than that of the legislators and their constituents who passed the legislation.

V

Roe and Abortion

The understanding of privacy advanced by *Griswold* enabled the overturning of laws against abortion. In 1973, a short eight years after *Griswold*, *Roe v. Wade* established a constitutional right to abortion.[1] States had begun to liberalize their abortion laws, and New York had made abortion available nearly on demand, but *Roe v. Wade* established a right to abortion that was more liberal than the laws of every state.[2]

What drove the effort to permit abortion? Advocates of abortion generally provided three justifications—the large number of illegal abortions, the need for therapeutic abortions, the fundamental right of women to privacy and liberty in reproductive decisions.[3] There is also considerable evidence that the widespread availability of contraception facilitated the exercise of sex outside of marriage, and therefore led to an increase in unwed pregnancies and abortions[4] (and divorces as well).[5] In fact, in virtually every country that possessed laws against abortion, its legalization quickly followed the widespread use of contraception.

Roe applied the right to privacy established in *Griswold* to abortion; indeed, *Roe* deemed abortion to be a fundamental right:

> The Court has recognized that a right of personal privacy, or a guarantee of certain areas or zones of privacy, does exist under the Constitution. ... Only personal rights that can be *deemed "fundamental" or "implicit in the concept of ordered liberty"* ... are included in this guarantee of personal privacy. ... This right of privacy, whether it be founded in the Fourteenth Amendment's concept of personal liberty and restrictions upon state action, as we feel it is, or, as the District Court determined, in the Ninth Amendment's reservation of rights to the people, is broad enough to encompass a woman's decision whether or not to terminate her pregnancy.[6]

Yet *Roe* also notes that the right to abortion is not an absolute right and that abortion could be regulated by the state for various reasons:

> On the basis of elements such as these, appellant and some amici argue that the woman's right is absolute and that she is entitled to terminate her pregnancy at whatever time, in whatever way, and for whatever reason she alone chooses. With this we do not agree. Appellant's arguments that Texas either has no valid interest at all in regulating the abortion decision, or no interest

strong enough to support any limitation upon the woman's sole determination, are unpersuasive. *The Court's decisions recognizing a right of privacy also acknowledge that some state regulation in areas protected by that right is appropriate.* As noted above, a State may properly assert important interests in safeguarding health, in maintaining medical standards, and in protecting potential life. At some point in pregnancy, these respective interests become sufficiently compelling to sustain regulation of the factors that govern the abortion decision. The privacy right involved, therefore, cannot be said to be absolute.[7]

Certainly all the reasons cited for regulating abortion were underlying the laws against abortion that *Roe* overturned. *Roe* decided that none of these interests was strong enough to trump a woman's right to abortion.

The way it dealt with the question of the humanity of the fetus is perhaps the most important question for, as the Court allows, if the fetus qualified as a human person, the fetus's right to life would trump the woman's right to privacy:

The appellee and certain amici argue that the fetus is a "person" within the language and meaning of the Fourteenth Amendment. In support of this, they outline at length and in detail the well-known facts of fetal development. *If this suggestion of personhood is established, the appellant's case, of course, collapses, for the fetus' right to life would then be guaranteed specifically* by the Amendment. The appellant conceded as much on reargument. On the other hand, the appellee conceded on reargument that no case could be cited that holds that a fetus is a person within the meaning of the Fourteenth Amendment.[8]

While it is not the point of this essay to argue for the humanity of the fetus, it is perhaps of interest to note that forces driving the attempts to make abortion legal were not related to some scientific discovery concerning the status of unborn human life. Rather, far from there being any scientific studies that revealed that past laws had been wrong to recognize the unborn as fully human, science increasingly ratified the humanity of the unborn. In April 1965, Lennart Nilsson's pictures of the unborn child in the womb featured in *Life Magazine* stunned the American public.[9]

In spite of overwhelming scientific evidence that human life begins at conception, *Roe* expressed agnosticism on the question of when human life begins. *Roe* claimed that the beginning of life was a matter impossible to establish, although some protection of the law might be permitted when the fetus was determined to be viable (a shifting standard to be sure).[10] This agnosticism might appear inexplicable given that medical textbooks for decades had straightforwardly noted that human life begins at conception and that a doctor who treats a pregnant woman has two patients, the pregnant woman and her unborn child.[11] Indeed, Sandra Day O'Connor noted some years later (in 1983) that the "*Roe* framework ...

is clearly on a collision course with itself" with respect to abortion:

> As the medical risks of various abortion procedures decrease, the point at which the State may regulate for reasons of maternal health is moved further forward to actual childbirth. As medical science becomes better able to provide for the separate existence of the fetus, the point of viability is moved further back toward conception.[12]

Increasingly, indifference to the life of the unborn child in the face of the freedom of the mother is clear; for instance, prominent feminists such as Naomi Wolf have acknowledged that abortion is the taking of a human life but insist that women should be permitted to do so.[13]

It is not clear what understanding of the right to privacy is operative in *Roe*.[14] Is it that the womb is a private place like the bedroom? *Griswold* spoke of the inviolability of the bedroom, but *Roe* does not cede that inviolability to the body. In fact, *Roe* explicitly denies the inviolability of the body:

> In fact, it is not clear to us that the claim asserted by some amici that one has an unlimited right to do with one's body as one pleases bears a close relationship to the right of privacy previously articulated in the Court's decisions. The Court has refused to recognize an unlimited right of this kind in the past.[15]

The denial here, though, seems directed toward the claim that there is an "unlimited" right to do with one's body as one wants, for the Court understands that in the past the law has mandated vaccinations and sterilizations—clearly, these are violations of bodily integrity, violations justified as protections of the good of the individual and the good of others.

Roe itself is surprisingly quiet about bodily integrity; rather, it invokes the right to privacy on the understanding that decisions of reproduction are those where self-determination is particularly important. The fullest statement can be found in the following paragraph:

> This right of privacy, whether it be founded in the Fourteenth Amendment's concept of personal liberty and restrictions upon state action, as we feel it is, or, as the District Court determined, in the Ninth Amendment's reservation of rights to the people, is broad enough to encompass a woman's decision whether or not to terminate her pregnancy. The detriment that the State would impose upon the pregnant woman by denying this choice altogether is apparent. Specific and direct harm medically diagnosable even in early pregnancy may be involved. Maternity, or additional offspring, may force upon the woman a distressful life and future. Psychological harm may be imminent. Mental and physical health may be taxed by child care. There is also the distress, for all concerned, associated with the unwanted child, and there is the problem of bringing a child into a family already unable, psychologically and otherwise, to care for it. In other cases, as in this

one, the additional difficulties and continuing stigma of unwed motherhood may be involved. All these are factors the woman and her responsible physician necessarily will consider in consultation.[16]

From this paragraph we can infer that the court believes that the decision to continue a pregnancy has such profound impact on a woman's life that it should properly be within the range of the decisions that should be the product of self-determination.

Planned Parenthood v. Casey (1992) further advanced the importance of the subjectivity of the individual.[17] Governor Robert Casey of Pennsylvania worked with state legislators to pass laws restricting abortion in some respects; for instance, the state required a twenty-four-hour waiting period for a woman seeking an abortion; it also required that a husband be informed of his wife's intention to have an abortion and that parents be informed of their minor daughter's intention to have an abortion. Opponents of abortion were hoping that the court would take the opportunity presented by *Casey* to revisit and overturn *Roe*. Rather than doing so, the case extended the principle of individual subjectivism in an unprecedented way.

Planned Parenthood v. Casey appealed to *Griswold* and *Roe* for the understanding of privacy advanced in that case, but also acknowledged an existential connection between contraception and abortion that now made abortion a practical necessity:

Abortion is customarily chosen as an unplanned response to the consequence of unplanned activity or to the failure of conventional birth control. ... For two decades of economic and social developments, people have organized intimate relationships and made choices that define their views of themselves and their places in society, in reliance on the availability of abortion in the event that contraception should fail.[18]

The Court clearly links the issues of abortion and contraception existentially: women need abortions because they engage in sexual relationships in which a pregnancy is not welcome.

Casey speaks more comfortably of liberty than of privacy, but it is clear that it has the right to privacy in mind:[19]

It should be recognized, moreover, that in some critical respects the abortion decision is of the same character as the decision to use contraception, to which *Griswold v. Connecticut, Eisenstadt v. Baird*, and *Carey v. Population Services International* afford constitutional protection. We have no doubt as to the correctness of those decisions. They support the reasoning in *Roe* relating to the *woman's liberty, because they involve personal decisions concerning not only the meaning of procreation but also human responsibility and respect for it.* As with abortion, reasonable people will have differences of opinion about these matters. One view is based on such reverence for the wonder of creation that any pregnancy ought to be welcomed and carried to full term no matter how difficult it will be to provide for the child and ensure its well-being. Another is that the inability to provide for the nurture and care of the infant is a cruelty to the child and an anguish to the parent. These are *intimate views with infinite variations,* and their deep, personal character underlay our decisions in *Griswold*, *Eisenstadt*, and *Carey*. The same concerns are present when the woman confronts the reality that, perhaps despite her attempts to avoid it, she has become pregnant.[20]

Although the greatest emphasis is on liberty, bodily integrity is invoked:

It is an inescapable biological fact that state regulation with respect to the child a woman is carrying will have a far greater impact on the mother's liberty than on the father's. The effect of state regulation on a woman's protected liberty is doubly deserving of scrutiny in such a case, as the State has touched not only upon the private sphere of the family but upon the very bodily integrity of the pregnant woman.[21]

Casey, in fact, references *Roe* as a source of understanding the body as protected by privacy rights:

Roe ... may be seen not only as an exemplar of *Griswold* liberty but as a rule (whether or not mistaken) of personal autonomy and bodily integrity, with doctrinal affinity to cases recognizing limits on governmental power to mandate medical treatment or to bar its rejection.[22]

Talk here of bodily integrity seems a bit imprecise, since such a claim would seem more properly to refer to what *cannot* be done to the body. Various invasions of the body are impermissible, whereas here it is being used to justify abortion, a fairly ferocious assault on two bodies—both that of the woman and that of the fetus. Strangely, pregnancy is seen as violating bodily integrity and abortion is not.

What really counts, however, is not bodily integrity but "personal autonomy"—the right to make decisions about matters such as marriage and procreation is elastically stretched by *Casey*: "At the heart of liberty is the right to define one's own concept of existence, of meaning, of the universe, and the mystery of human life."[23] This passage reflects the individualism and skepticism that leads to relativism. It suggests that there is no meaning to reality that we all must discover and live by; rather, it states that we are to be free to define—not to discover, but to define—the meaning of existence. Now *Casey* does not explicitly say that we are all free to define when human life begins; in fact, *Casey* emphatically did not want to revisit the question when human life or personhood begins; rather, it reiterated a conviction that "viability" was a suitable marker point for possible state protection of life. Yet, the astonishing link that *Casey* made between contraception and abortion in the passage cited above allows that the use of contraception and the decision to have abortions are "personal decisions." Read in light of the "heart of liberty" clause, it is not so far-fetched to think that the decision of when human life begins—at least within some range of possibility, say, up to viability—is not a matter to be decided by scientific evidence but by personal values.

VI

ASSISTED SUICIDE
AND HOMOSEXUALITY

At the time of *Roe,* some predicted that its reasoning guaranteed that assisted suicide and euthanasia would eventually become legal.[1] Once thought to be scaremongers, they now seem prophetic, since the courts have repeatedly made explicit connections between cases that deal with reproductive issues and end-of-life issues. *Casey* has become a commanding precedent for "right to die" cases. The logic is simple: if, as *Casey* asserts, we have the right to decide who qualifies as human in accord with our own subjective preferences, then it seems that we should also be able to decide when our own lives are worth living and when they are not. As we will see, *Compassion in Dying v. Washington* (1996) uses *Casey*'s "heart of liberty" passage to make just that claim.[2] Stated even more boldly, if a woman's right to her own body extends to the right to kill a child within her, why would she not have a right to kill herself?

Whereas the Supreme Court designated contraception and abortion as *fundamental rights*, in two cases, *Vacco v. Quill* (1997) and *Washington v. Glucksberg* (1997),[3] the Court refused to recognize assisted suicide as a *fundamental right* meriting constitutional protection, and resolved rather that it is a *liberty interest* and that states are free to decide its legality.[4] Fundamental rights are those that cannot be abrogated by the law; the liberty interests of individuals must sometimes yield to the interests of the state. The refusal of the courts to recognize assisted suicide as a fundamental right disturbs advocates of abortion, who argue that the continued protection of reproductive autonomy requires recognizing a *right* to assisted suicide.[5] Many feminists find *Vacco* and *Glucksberg* so threatening in what seems to be a restriction of privacy concerns that they urge a reframing of the terms of the debate: they argue that abortion advocates might better resort to appeals to gender equality rather than privacy to ensure continued access to abortion.[6] Yet, while that strategy may eventually be adopted, court cases involving end-of-life decisions regularly cite the set of privacy rights or liberty interests invoked in such cases as *Griswold*, *Roe*, and *Casey*.

In fact, there is a clear mutual dependency between cases dealing with reproductive issues and cases dealing with end-of-life issues. Cases dealing with end-of-life issues depend upon contraception and abortion cases, and cases dealing with contraception and abortion depend upon end-of-life cases.[7] For instance, in one of the first cases to assert a right to refuse medical treatment, *In re Quinlan* (1976),[8] the New Jersey State Supreme Court found justification for this right in *Griswold* and *Roe*:

> The Court in *Griswold* found the unwritten constitutional right of privacy to exist in the penumbra of specific guarantees of the Bill of Rights "formed by emanations from those guarantees that help give them life and substance." ... Presumably this right is broad enough to encompass a patient's decision to decline medical treatment under certain circumstances, in much the same way as it is broad enough to encompass a woman's decision to terminate pregnancy under certain conditions. *Roe v. Wade* ... (1973).[9]

Further discussion of Karen Quinlan's right to privacy speaks of her treatment as involving "minimal bodily invasion" but found that her dismal prognosis made even that invasion a violation of privacy: "We think that the State's interest contra weakens and the individual's right to privacy grows as the degree of bodily invasion increases and the prognosis dims."[10] The strange talk of a right to privacy "growing" as a "prognosis dims" —used here to defend cessation of treatment—is perhaps an eerie precursor to the claim that those who are terminally ill should have access to assisted suicide.

Karen's incompetence to exercise her right did not abrogate her right:

> If a putative decision by Karen to permit this non-cognitive, vegetative existence to

terminate by natural forces is regarded as
a valuable incident of her right of privacy,
as we believe it to be, then it should not
be discarded solely on the basis that her
condition prevents her conscious exercise
of the choice.[11]

Karen's parents were permitted to exercise her
right for her. (Let me note that I believe it was moral
to discontinue use of the respirator, because its
use constituted extraordinary care and thus was
not obligatory. What I dispute is that the "right to
privacy" justified the discontinuance.)

A later case, *Compassion in Dying* (1996,
Ninth Circuit Court of Appeals), in seeking to
legalize assisted suicide, explicitly acknowledges
its dependence upon the principles established in
abortion and contraception cases:

Because they present issues of such profound spiritual importance and because
they so deeply affect individuals' right to
determine their own destiny, the abortion
and right-to-die cases have given rise to
a highly emotional and divisive debate. In
many respects, the legal arguments on both
sides are similar, as are the constitutional
principles at issue.

In deciding right-to-die cases, we are guided
by the Court's approach to the abortion
cases. *Casey* in particular provides a powerful precedent, for in that case the Court
had the opportunity to evaluate its past decisions and to determine whether to adhere
to its original judgment. Although *Casey*
was influenced by the doctrine of *stare de-*

cisis [honoring precedent], the fundamental message of that case lies in its statements regarding the type of issue that confronts us here: "These matters, involving the most intimate and personal choices a person may make in a lifetime, choices central to personal dignity and autonomy, are central to the liberty protected by the Fourteenth Amendment."[12]

Early in the majority opinion of *Compassion in Dying* we find the assertion that "every man has the liberty to determine the time and manner of his death." Note that there are no limitations in this statement—it is not limited to the imminently dying or even the terminally ill. Indeed, there is no logic to limiting the "right to die" only to those near death or in intolerable pain.[13] Since state permission to kill ourselves is based on privacy or autonomy, why should we not be permitted to determine for ourselves when our lives are not worth living—why do we need the state to make this determination for us?

Compassion in Dying, in seeking to establish assisted suicide as a right, invokes contraception and abortion cases and the right to privacy.[14] By portraying both Socrates and Christ as "suicides," the justices dub suicide a time-honored liberty in spite of the fact that neither nations nor states have ever recognized that citizens can kill themselves when they choose.[15] The justices seem innocent of Socrates' denial that his drinking the hemlock could be construed as suicide: indeed, in the *Phaedo* (62C), Plato's dialogue about Socrates' death, Socrates argues that suicide is wrong precisely because life is a gift from God and it is wrong to reject that gift. The later assisted-suicide cases, *Vacco* and *Glucksberg*, had a better sense of history. In repudiating assisted suicide as a protected constitutional right, they cite the long history of laws against assisted suicide and reject *Compassion's* reading of the historical record.

Yet we must admit that the reasoning of *Compassion* sounds unassailable to our modern ears—for surely we own our bodies and our lives are ours to do with as we please, are they not? In this reasoning we see clearly what radical autonomy and radical individualism mean and how commonsensical this radical break with tradition has become for us. The idea that our lives are to be put at the service of others and that suicide would almost certainly mean abdicating some if not most of our responsibilities and obligations is entirely absent from the decision and is, in fact, a fairly novel idea to many who live in twenty-first-century America.

New rights have emerged alongside the right to privacy to facilitate approval of assisted suicide: *Cruzan v. Director, MDH* (1990),[16] a case that permitted the withdrawal of artificial nutrition and hydration from a woman in a persistent vegetative state, catalogues a long list of court cases approving withdrawal of treatment, sometimes on the basis of "privacy" but also on such rights as the "right to informed consent" or the "right to self-determination." Thus, one line of "logic" developing from *Griswold* to *Roe*, from *Roe* to *Casey*, and from *Casey* to *Compassion* is clear: If couples have the right to do in the bedroom what they want, a woman has a right to do with her body what she wants. If a woman has the right to kill the fetus growing within, she has the right to kill herself.

Only Oregon has responded to the Supreme Court's decision that assisted suicide is a liberty to be granted individual states by passing a "Death with Dignity Act." Yet, in spite of little explicit legal recognition of the "right to die" in American jurisprudence, the work of authors such as Wesley Smith show how common it is in medical practice to hasten the death of one's patients, whether by withdrawing hydration or nutrition or by declaring some treatment futile.[17] There seems to be a kind of de facto practice of euthanasia in modern American medicine.

The right to privacy's marathon run seemed to hit a bit of a pothole when the Supreme Court in *Bowers v. Hardwick* (1986) emphatically denied that the right to privacy could be invoked to protect homosexual acts of sexual intercourse.[18] It was just a small setback, however, because seventeen years later it got back on its feet when *Lawrence v. Texas* (2003) ruled that laws against homosexual acts were unconstitutional.[19]

Both the decision in *Bowers* and its overturning by *Lawrence* can be legitimately described as astonishing. Gay and lesbian groups had the reasonable expectation that the Court would extend the right to privacy to protect homosexual acts and thus were disappointed by *Bowers*.[20] What makes the overturning of *Bowers* remarkable is its defiant rejection of *Casey*'s commitment to *stare decisis*, the principle that precedence should be honored. That principle was invoked in *Casey* as the reason the Court could not allow the possibility of overturning *Roe*, which was then some twenty years old. In *Lawrence*, the Court decided that *stare decisis* did not apply, even though there were only seventeen years between *Bowers* and *Lawrence*; Justice Scalia in his dissenting opinion accused the Court of being manipulative and selective in its employment of the principle. Evidently, three years of longevity makes all the difference in precedential power.

Lawrence recited the usual litany of "privacy" cases—*Griswold*, *Eisenstadt*, *Roe*, and *Casey*—as a prelude to its own decision that laws against homosexual acts are unconstitutional. The conclusion of *Lawrence* reflects the themes of this essay:

> Liberty protects the person from unwarranted government intrusions into a dwelling or other *private* places. In our tradition the State is not omnipresent in the home. And there are other spheres of our lives and existence, outside the home, where the State should not be a dominant presence. Freedom extends beyond spatial bounds. Liberty presumes an autonomy of self that includes freedom of thought, belief, expression, and certain intimate conduct. The instant case involves liberty of the person both in its *spatial* and *more transcendent dimensions*.[21]

Here we see the dual understanding of the right to privacy that has been weaving through Court decisions, both the view that certain places are private (one wonders if bathhouses and public restrooms are included and cannot be intruded upon by the government). "Privacy" has also become a code word for autonomy and the right to "define one's own concept of existence, and meaning." Not surprisingly, the famous "heart of liberty" clause from *Casey* is cited in *Lawrence*.

While the signers of the opinion in *Lawrence* denied that *Lawrence* paves the way for recognition of same-sex marriages, that assurance carries no more weight than the assurance of *Griswold* that its reasoning would not pave the way for the legalization of homosexuality. Justice Scalia characteristically minced no words in predicting that *Bowers* "effectively decrees the end of all morals legislation," such as laws against "fornication, bigamy, adultery, adult incest, bestiality, and obscenity." He went further and predicted an inevitable recognition of same-sex marriages, in spite of the adamant denial of the majority that *Bowers* would entail their recognition. The fact that in 2003, the Supreme Judicial Court of Massachusetts ruled that same-sex couples have the right to marry might rightly be seen as swift confirmation of Scalia's prophecy.[22] Recent attempts to secure legal recognition of polygamous marriages indicates that the "right to privacy" is still very much in the lead in the marathon it is running.

VII

POLITICAL CONNECTIONS AND NATURAL CONSEQUENCES

Judicial decisions clearly establish links between contraception, abortion, assisted suicide, and homosexual acts. At the outset I suggested various philosophical assumptions that explain the proliferation of rights in the modern age, especially rights to actions whose justification is based largely on the exaltation of individual autonomy and a commitment to relativism. Here I will take a quick look at some of the political and "lifestyle" connections between these issues.

As mentioned earlier, Protestant legislatures in the nineteenth century, on both national and state levels, passed legislation against contraception. Abortion, assisted suicide, and homosexual acts were also illegal throughout the United States until very recently. The laws against contraception were attacked first. Both those promoting liberalization of laws against contraception and those opposing it saw connections between contraception, abortion, euthanasia, and homosexuality.

A quick review of the history of the positions of Margaret Sanger and Planned Parenthood serves to paint a picture of the connected advocacy for the legalization of these issues. Margaret Sanger, founder of organizations that were precursors to Planned Parenthood, was a zealous opponent of laws against contraception and also a founding member of the Euthanasia Society of America.[1] This may have been a position she took for political reasons; she was notoriously capable of taking positions because they were conducive to her foremost goal: the legalization of contraception.[2] Sanger was a committed eugenicist and advocate for forced sterilization of the "unfit," which included both the deformed and the poor, particularly African Americans and Catholic immigrants.[3] While Sanger herself did not advocate for abortion (the possibility of legalizing abortion in her time was nonexistent), Planned Parenthood is now the single largest provider of abortion services in the United States. It is also a firm advocate of the rights of homosexuals, including the right to marry.[4]

To trace the connections between contraception, abortion, assisted suicide, and eugenics is beyond the scope of this book, but the following should be mentioned in passing. The eugenics movement advanced by Margaret Sanger and many other luminaries of her time is basically dead in the United States, a movement that was directed toward reducing the number of African Americans, the disabled, the poor, and the mentally handicapped through such means as mandatory sterilization, which was once legal in the United States.[5] Eugenics may no longer be necessary, because several of its goals have been achieved through abortion practices. Abortion has been used to greatly reduce the number of babies born with Down syndrome, for instance, and the high rate of abortion among African Americans has led some to speak of it as black genocide.[6]

Perhaps it should not be surprising that the Catholic Church has long fought the legalization of contraception, abortion, assisted suicide, and homosexuality. The Catholic Church on many levels was a ferocious opponent of Margaret Sanger, Planned Parenthood, and all efforts to legalize contraception.[7] Bishops, theologians, the Catholic media, and Catholic laity mobilized in many ways to combat those efforts.[8] In the 1920s, Archbishop Patrick Hayes twice debated Margaret Sanger in the pages of the *New York Times*.[9] In 1924, Catholic Boy Scouts distributed a pamphlet against contraception at a birth control conference in Syracuse.[10] In 1931, *Commonweal* magazine warned that greater access to contraceptives would lead to "state clinics for abortion."[11] In 1948, an influential Jesuit priest, John Ford, stated that arguments used to promote contraception were also being advanced to promote "mercy killings."[12] For decades, Catholics heard regular homilies from their priests on the immorality of contraception and to a large extent embraced those teachings and happily had large families. The Church also lobbied hard against initiatives of the government to make contraceptives available to the military, to welfare recipients, and as a part of overseas aid programs.[13]

In the 1960s, Catholics began to drop their support of laws against contraception. Reasons for the diminishment of Catholic support for these laws range from Catholic interest in assimilating into the broader culture to Catholic dependence on funding from the Great Society initiatives in the 1960s and a sense that a defeat was inevitable.[14] Another significant factor was the influence of the famous Jesuit John Courtney Murray, who argued that contraception should not be proscribed by the law since the use of contraception is a private matter.[15] He influenced high churchmen such as Cardinal Cushing in New York and at least one Supreme Court Justice; his position, in fact, was quoted in *Poe v. Ullman*, a Supreme Court case that was the precursor to *Griswold*.[16] Indeed, some prominent Catholics, such as Rev. Theodore Hesburgh, president of Notre Dame, through his involvement with the Rockefeller Commission, may have been indispensable in promoting the growing acceptance of contraception as a solution to the perceived population problem.[17]

Concerning the Catholic retreat from the battlefield on contraception in Connecticut, Catholic historian John McGreevy observed that "one can hardly imagine a less propitious beginning for Catholic opposition to the relaxation of restrictions against abortion."[18] Rev. Brian Hehir, advisor to the bishops, recommended that they abandon opposition to government policies that would promote contraception. His efforts

> would produce such controversy within the NCCB and the USCC secretariat that the weary leaders of the conference would gradually demote abortion from its place as the most pressing public policy matter affecting American life.[19]

Indeed, the Church in the United States became so nonzealous about the teaching on contraception that not only did it withdraw from supporting laws against contraception, for the most part it also withdrew from urging its own members to follow the teaching. From 1966 until 2006, the bishops of the United States, as a corporate body, issued not a single statement defending the Church's teaching on contraception, with the exception of a statement commemorating the twenty-fifth anniversary of *Humanae vitae*.[20] In earlier decades the Church had found many ways to promulgate the teaching.[21] Although the U.S. bishops have been in the forefront of fighting for the lives of the unborn from the start, they have never regained the influence in the public sphere they had before *Griswold*. It is unlikely that with the trajectory of modern culture they could have retained that influence, but their voluntary withdrawal from the battlefield may have hastened the diminution of their power and made them less effective in their defense of the unborn.

There are signs in recent decades that the U.S. bishops, both individually and corporately, are willing to engage the culture aggressively on other life issues in addition to abortion. One notable success was the opposition of the Catholic

Church in Michigan to Proposal B in 1998, a proposal to make assisted suicide legal. Just weeks before the vote, the proposal was overwhelmingly expected to pass, and the turn-around is largely credited to Catholic involvement.[22] Another example is the aggressive opposition to allowing same-sex couples to marry and adopt children; for instance, the U.S. bishops have expressed support of the Marriage Protection Amendment.[23] Sometimes the Church—and culture—has paid a big price for heroic loyalty to Catholic principle: the Archdiocese of Boston withdrew from providing adoption services rather than place children in homes of homosexual couples.[24] But, after all, we were promised that there would be big crosses to bear in this world.

We have seen that fundamental philosophical presuppositions, judicial decisions, and political action unite contraception, abortion, assisted suicide, and homosexual acts. There are several kinds of logic that unite these practices, but one is the logic of natural consequences. Since contraception is a rejection of children and also a cause of unwed pregnancy, contraception both logically and naturally leads to abortion. The practice of abortion—killing when life is inconvenient—logically leads to assisted suicide. Contraception has associations with homosexuality. Since contraception legitimizes sex that excludes the procreative possibility, logically it leads to approval of homosexual sex. Homosexuality also lends some force to the push for assisted suicide, since homosexuals with AIDS are the group that has the highest incidence of suicide and requests for physician-assisted suicide.[25] The connection between these issues is not simply theoretical; it is causal.

Evangelium vitae identifies the connection between several of these issues. *Evangelium vitae* speaks of contraception and abortion as being the "fruits of the same tree" and states:

> It is true that in many cases contraception and even abortion are practiced under the pressure of real-life difficulties, which nonetheless can never exonerate from striving to observe God's law fully. Still, in very many other instances such practices are rooted in a hedonistic mentality unwilling to accept responsibility in matters of sexuality, and they imply a self-centered concept of freedom, which regards procreation as an obstacle to personal fulfilment. The life which could result from a sexual encounter thus becomes an enemy to be avoided at all costs, and abortion becomes the only possible decisive response to failed contraception. (n.13)

Throughout, *Evangelium vitae* notes that in our culture reproductive issues and end-of-life issues are regularly linked; for instance, it speaks of the role of the media:

> Nor can it be denied that the mass media are often implicated in this conspiracy, by lending credit to that culture which presents recourse to contraception, sterilization, abortion, and even euthanasia as a mark of progress and a victory of freedom, while depicting as enemies of freedom and prog-

ress those positions which are unreservedly
pro-life. (n. 17)

It also speaks of the role of the state:

> The State is no longer the "common home"
> where all can live together on the basis of
> principles of fundamental equality, but is
> transformed into a tyrant State, which ar-
> rogates to itself the right to dispose of the
> life of the weakest and most defenseless
> members, from the unborn child to the el-
> derly, in the name of a public interest which
> is really nothing but the interest of one part.
> The appearance of the strictest respect for
> legality is maintained, at least when the
> laws permitting abortion and euthanasia
> are the result of a ballot in accordance
> with what are generally seen as the rules
> of democracy. Really, what we have here is
> only the tragic caricature of legality; the
> democratic ideal, which is only truly such
> when it acknowledges and safeguards the
> dignity of every human person, is betrayed
> in its very foundations. (n. 20)

While the legalization of abortion was not directly
the result of a ballot in the United States, it can
be said to be the result of democracy, since duly
elected officials appoint the judges, who argued
that they were promoting liberty in legalizing
abortion.

Still, as I have mentioned, I think it is argu-
able that abortion was found constitutional not
primarily because of a deeper understanding of
the right to privacy or because of a desire to advance the rights of women, but because abortion

had become necessary in light of the number of unwed pregnancies that followed the widespread use of contraception. Earlier, we considered these claims from *Casey*:

> In some critical respects, the abortion decision is of the same character as the decision to use contraception. ... For two decades of economic and social developments, [people] have organized intimate relationships and made choices that define their views of themselves and their places in society, in reliance on the availability of abortion in the event that contraception should fail.[26]

As the Supreme Court candidly states, we need abortion so that we can continue our contraceptive lifestyles. It rather clearly implies that as long as we are a contraceptive culture we must be an abortive culture. And let us not think that the primary problem is the failure rate of contraceptives—that if contraceptives were more reliable then abortions would go away. Contraceptive failure surely plays a role, but primarily women are seeking abortions because they are having sexual intercourse with men with whom they are not prepared to have babies—and clearly contraception facilitates that act. Many men and women simply do not use contraceptives responsibly—in fact, 50 percent of women who have abortions were not using a contraceptive when they got pregnant, although they were contraceptively experienced. Even if contraceptives were 100 percent effective, it is unlikely that individuals would be so responsible that they would always use them when a pregnancy was not desirable.

Contraception leads to unwed pregnancy, unwed pregnancy leads to abortion, and abortion leads to the devaluation of human life. If we can take the lives of the unborn when they are inconvenient to us, then logically we should be able to take our own lives when they are inconvenient to us. Moreover, we may soon be clamoring not just for assisted suicide but for euthanasia as well. Contraception and abortion lead to smaller families, and thus the burden of caring for the ill and for elderly parents or relatives is not something one can share with other siblings. As Charles Rice has observed,

> We should not be surprised when the secular, contraceptive society turns to euthanasia as a remedy for the financial and other problems caused by the increasing proportion of old people, which itself is a result of contraception and abortion.[27]

Let us not doubt that, at this moment, more and more individuals in compromised states, who are thus inconvenient to others, are having their health care discontinued or managed in such a way as to cause or hasten their deaths. The highly publicized case of Terri Schiavo is surely not an isolated instance.

The connections between contraception and homosexuality are interesting. Theoretically, the view that sex does not need to honor its procreative meaning goes a long way to legitimizing homosexual sex. The nearly universal view that sexual intercourse pursued strictly for pleasure and with no regard for a procreative orientation has surely led to the widespread acceptance of homosexuality and the advocacy of homosexual marriage. Another possible connection is between the phenomenon of contraception and increased unwed parenthood and divorces. Fathers of boys who grow up in single parent households are often "absent" from their sons' lives. Young boys whose fathers are absent from their lives are at greater risk of becoming homosexuals.[28] Not only boys, of course, suffer from the lack of a loving father in the home; the damage is more widespread. Presently, about 36 percent of babies are born to single mothers. Nearly 70 percent of children born in the United States will live with single mothers or in households touched by divorce. Children raised in single-parent households are much more likely to be poor and to suffer a host of ills, such a depression and addiction.[29]

The degeneration of morality and the quality of life for children can be attributed a great deal to the acceptance of contraception, abortion, assisted suicide, and homosexuality. We have seen the courts invent new rights, apply legitimate rights in distorted ways, and ignore facts and natural relationships to protect actions and lifestyles that are destructive of important human goods and even the most basic of goods, human life. Understanding what cultural phenomena and philosophies drive the Culture of Death should make us better prepared to be advocates for the Culture of Life.

NOTES

Chapter I
Culture Wars

1. John Paul II, *Evangelium vitae* (March 25, 1995), n. 18, http://www.vatican.va/.

2. Ibid. See, in particular, nn. 18–24.

3. I will use "assisted suicide" and "euthanasia" somewhat interchangeably throughout. The Church considers assisted suicide one form of euthanasia. Currently, it is the only form of euthanasia that is legal in the United States, and only in Oregon.

4. Many books and articles attempt to describe the competing fundamental principles in the cultural wars; see, for instance, James Davison Hunter, *Cultural Wars: The Struggle to Define America* (New York: Basic Books, 1991); Robert Bork, *Slouching Towards Gomorrah: Modern Liberalism and America's Decline* (New York: Harper Collins, 1996); Charles Rice, *The Winning Side* (Mishawaka, IN: St. Brendan's Institute, 1999); and Robert P. George, *The Clash of Orthodoxies: Law, Morality and Religion in Crisis* (Wilmington, DE: Intercollegiate Studies Institute, 2001).

5. Peter Singer, *Practical Ethics*, 2nd ed. (Cambridge, U.K.: Cambridge University Press, 1999).

6. Here I use the term "intrinsic worth" in a more traditional sense than does Dworkin and others. By "intrinsic worth" I mean to say that an entity that has intrinsic worth is of more than instrumental value; it has a meaning and value of its own without reference to further value. Human life, in fact, is the only embodied life of intrinsic worth, though not the only reality or value of intrinsic worth (virtues and beauty, for instance, have intrinsic worth). Such life is truly inviolable—that is, it is never of subordinate value to other goods and can never be the object of direct and deliberate killing. Dworkin and others maintain that, though of "intrinsic worth" and "inviolable," human life can be directly and deliberately attacked. Our terminology differs radically. Ronald Dworkin, *Life's Dominion: An Argument about Abortion, Euthanasia, and Individual Freedom* (New York: Vintage Books, 1993). For a devastating review of Dworkin, see Gerard V. Bradley, "Life's Dominion: A Review Essay," *Notre Dame Law Review* 69.2 (1993): 380–385.

7. For an excellent review of these positions, see Renée Mirkes, O.S.F., "NBAC and Embryo Ethics," *National Catholic Bioethics Quarterly* 1.2 (Summer 2001): 163–187.

8. A current treatment of those differences can be found in George, *Clash of Orthodoxies*, 2.

9. For a thorough critique of the U.N. assault on human rights through the advocacy of reproductive rights, see Douglas A. Sylva, "United Nations Population Fund: Assault on the World's Peoples," white paper, published by Catholic Family and Human Rights Institute, 2002, http://www.c-fam.org.

10. The use of "privacy" to advance autonomy has been much criticized as well as defended. For an introduction to the debate, see Richard C. Turkington and

Notes

Anita L. Allen, eds., *Privacy Law: Cases and Materials* (St. Paul, MN: West Group, 1999), 609 to end; Ferdinand David Schoeman, ed., *The Philosophical Dimensions of Privacy* (Cambridge, U.K.: Cambridge University Press, 1984); and, of course, Lawrence H. Tribe, "Rights of Privacy and Personhood," in *American Constitutional Law*, 2nd ed. (New York: Foundation Press, 1988). See also Tribe's *Abortion: The Clash of Absolutes* (New York: Norton, 1990). For an argument that the Constitution properly allows no constitutional right to an abortion, see John Noonan, *A Private Choice: Abortion in America in the Seventies* (New York: Free Press, 1979). For a critique of the use of the "right to privacy" to justify abortion, see Lynn D. Wardle, *The Abortion Privacy Doctrine: A Compendium and Critique of Federal Court Abortion Cases* (Buffalo, NY: William S. Hein, 1980) and his "Rethinking *Roe v. Wade*," *Brigham Young University Law Review* 1985.2 (1985): 231–264. For an online review of legal cases involving the right to privacy, see http://members.aol.com/abtrbng/conlaw.htm.

11. *Lawrence v. Texas*, 539 U.S. 558 (2003). Unless otherwise noted, all the court cases cited here are available at http://caselaw.lp.findlaw.com.

12. "The laws which, in many countries on the Continent, forbid marriage unless the parties can show that they have the means of supporting a family, do not exceed the legitimate powers of the State: and whether such laws be expedient or not (a question mainly dependent on local circumstances and feelings), they are not objectionable as violations of liberty." John Stuart Mill, *On Liberty and Other Essays* (New York: Oxford University Press, 1998), 120.

Chapter II
A Distorted Understanding of Rights

1. I expand on this point in "Natural Law and Personalism in *Veritatis Splendor*," *Veritatis Splendor:*

American Responses, eds. Michael E. Allsopp and John J. O'Keefe (Kansas City, MO: Sheed & Ward, 1995), 194–207, reprinted in *John Paul II and Moral Theology: Readings in Moral Theology*, no. 10, eds. Charles E. Curran and Richard A. McCormick, S.J. (New York: Paulist Press, 1998), 67–84. File versions of my articles are available online at http://www.aodonline.org/SHMS/Faculty+5819/Janet+Smith+9260/Dr.+Janet+Smith+-+Published+Articles.htm.

2. I explore other options to rights language in moral discourse in "The Moral Vision of the Catechism," in *Evangelizing for the Third Millennium: The Maynooth Conference on the New Catechism*, May 1996, eds. Maurice Hogan, S.S.C., and Thomas J. Norris (Dublin: Veritatis Publications, 1997), 96–114.

3. *Griswold v. Connecticut*, 381 U.S. 479 (1965).

4. *Meachum v. Fano*, 427 U.S. 215, 230 (1976). This case deals with the transference of a prison from one facility to another.

5. For an argument that natural law justifications are unavoidable, especially in U.S. constitutional jurisprudence, see Russell Hittinger, "Liberalism and the American Natural Law Tradition," *Wake Forest Law Review* 25.3 (1990): 429–499.

6. See *Hill v. Colorado*, 530 U.S. 703 (2000).

7. See for instance, John T. Noonan, Jr., "An Almost Absolute Value in History," in *The Morality of Abortion: Legal and Historical Perspectives* (Cambridge, MA: Harvard University Press, 1970), 51–59.

8. Mary Ann Glendon, *Rights Talk: The Impoverishment of Political Discourse* (New York: Free Press, 1991), 14. See also her *Abortion and Divorce in Western Law* (Cambridge, MA: Harvard University Press, 1987) for an argument that U.S. law is significantly more subjective in these matters than European law. My work in this area owes a great deal to Glendon's books.

9. Well known is the argument of Judith Jarvis Thompson, "A Defense of Abortion," which speaks of the fetus as an uninvited intruder. *Philosophy and Public Affairs* 1.1 (1971): 47–66.

Chapter III
The Right to Privacy

1. Judith Jarvis Thompson, "The Right to Privacy," in Schoeman, *Philosophical Dimensions of Privacy*, 272.

2. Urinating and defecating are not private activities in all cultures; having sexual intercourse in private is nearly a universal value but not at all an activity that is seen as protected by the "space" of the bedroom. For reviews of sociological and anthropological studies, see Robert F. Murphy, "Social Distance and the Veil," 34–55, and Alan Westin, "The Origins of Modern Claims to Privacy," 56–74, in Schoeman, *Philosophical Dimensions of Privacy*.

3. John Hart Ely, an advocate of the legalization of abortion, observed that "what is frightening about *Roe* is that this super-protected right is not inferable from the language of the Constitution, the framers' thinking respecting the specific problem in issue, any general value derivable from the provisions they included, or the nation's governmental structure." "The Wages of Crying Wolf: A Comment on *Roe v. Wade*," *Yale Law Journal* 82 (1973): 935–936.

4. Glendon, *Rights Talk*, 21. Glendon explains that Locke "seems to have expected his readers to accept without question that proprietorship of one's body was a God-given right, as natural as breathing. That this proposition is less self-evident than Locke maintained, however, is apparent from the fact that continental Europeans find the notion startling, accustomed as they are to another idea, fundamental to their legal

systems, that a human body is not subject to ownership by anyone."

5. Ibid., 23.

6. This is a theme throughout Glendon's book, but see especially pp. 40–46, in her chapter titled "The Illusion of Absoluteness."

7. Again, Glendon makes fascinating comparisons between U.S. and European law; she notes that England "has never made privacy the subject of a general 'right'" (48).

8. Ibid., 40.

9. Ibid., 51.

10. Schoeman anthologizes some of the classic articles on privacy in *The Philosophical Dimensions of Privacy*.

11. Samuel D. Warren and Louis D. Brandeis, "The Right to Privacy," *Harvard Law Review* 4.5 (December 15, 1890): 193–220, available in Schoeman, *Philosophical Dimensions of Privacy*, 75–103, and at www.ucdmc. ucdavis.edu/compliance/guidance/privacy/privacy-right.html.

12. Ibid., emphasis added.

13. It is notable that contraception, abortion, and assisted suicide go virtually without mention in Schoeman, *Philosophical Dimensions of Privacy*, and occupy surprisingly little space in Turkington and Allen, *Privacy Law*.

14. Edward J. Bloustein, "Privacy as an Aspect of Human Dignity: An Answer to Dean Prosser," in Schoeman, *Philosophical Dimensions of Privacy*, 162.

15. Dean Prosser claims that "right to privacy" is a cluster term for four different kinds of torts that are "tied together by a common name, but otherwise have almost nothing in common except that each represents an interference with the right of the plaintiff ... 'to be

let alone.'" The four torts are these: (1) intrusion upon the plaintiff's seclusion or solitude, or into his private affairs; (2) public disclosure of embarrassing private facts about the plaintiff; (3) publicity which places the plaintiff in a false light in the public eye; and (4) appropriation, for the defendant's advantage, of the plaintiff's name or likeness. William L. Prosser, "Privacy" [a legal analysis], in Schoeman, *Philosophical Dimensions of Privacy*, 107. Bloustein challenges Prosser's readings of Warren and Brandeis and relevant cases: he argues that the relevant concept in Warren and Brandeis is their reference to the "inviolate personality," which he understands to be a principle that posits "the individual's independence, dignity and integrity; it defines man's essence as a unique and self-determining being." Bloustein, "Privacy as an Aspect of Human Dignity," 163.

16. See Prosser, "Privacy."

17. Ibid., 107 to end.

18. See Bloustein, "Privacy as an Aspect of Human Dignity."

19. *Compassion in Dying v. Washington*, 79 F.3d 790 (U.S. Ninth Circuit, 1996).

20. *Evangelium vitae* makes this point in n. 22.

21. Several essays in Schoeman, *Philosophical Dimensions of Privacy*, speculate about these needs.

Chapter IV
Griswold *and Contraception*

1. In a defense of Connecticut's laws against contraception before the Connecticut Supreme Court in 1939, state attorney Bill Fitzgerald argued that what was at stake here was "the constitutionally permissible purpose of preventing immorality, discouraging promiscuous sexual intercourse … promoting the public morals … protecting purity, preserving chastity, encourag-

ing chastity, encouraging continence and self-restraint, defending the sanctity of the home," and "lessening the incidence of the commission of the crime of abortion by those persons married or single who would otherwise be encouraged by the dubious and unproven but supposed power of artificial contraceptives to defeat the process of nature," cited in David J. Garrow, *Liberty and Sexuality: The Right to Privacy and the Making of* Roe v. Wade (Berkeley: University of California Press, 1998), 75.

2. Charles D. Provan, *The Bible and Birth Control* (Monongahela, PA: Zimmer, 1989).

3. The classic history of the Church's condemnation of contraception is John T. Noonan's *Contraception* (Cambridge, MA: Belknap, 1986, originally published in 1965). See also Leslie Woodcock Tentler, *Catholics and Contraception: An American History* (Ithaca, NY: Cornell University Press, 2004). Although both books were written in service of promoting a change in Church teaching on contraception, arguably they make a strong case for retaining the teaching. See my review of Tentler, "Good History, Bad Argument" in *First Things* (August/September 2005): 47–49.

4. For a good, brief recounting of this story, see Ralph McInerny, *What Went Wrong with Vatican II: The Catholic Crisis Explained* (Manchester, NH: Sophia Institute Press, 1998).

5. Russell Shorto, "Contra-contraception," *New York Times Magazine*, May 7, 2006.

6. See Francis Fukuyama, *The Great Disruption: Human Nature and the Reconstitution of the Social Order* (New York: Free Press, 2000); Lionel Tiger, *The Decline of Males* (New York: Golden Books Publishing Co., Inc., 1999); and my article *"Humanae Vitae*: A Prophetic Document?" *Respect Life*, the annual Respect Life publication for the U.S. bishops; reprinted in *Crisis* 6.8 (September 1988): 30–35. See also W. Bradford

Wilcox, "The Facts of Life and Marriage," *Touchstone* (January/February 2005).

7. Russell Hittinger, "Abortion Before *Roe*," *First Things* 46 (October 1994): 15.

8. It is of some interest that the attempt to challenge the constitutionality of the anti-contraceptive laws of Connecticut failed in *Poe v. Ullman* 367 U.S. 497 (1961). Many elements of Justice Douglas's decision found their way into *Griswold*; he spoke of the right to privacy and of emanations of liberty.

9. A perhaps too detailed account of this struggle can be found in Garrow, *Liberty and Sexuality*, 37.

10. For a succinct review of the attempt to legalize contraception, see Hittinger, "Abortion Before *Roe*," 14–23, and Robert P. George and David L. Tubbs, "The Bad Decision That Started It All," *National Review* (July 18, 2005): 39–40.

11. The relevant portion of the Fourteenth Amendment states that "no state shall make or enforce any law which shall abridge the privileges or immunities of citizens of the United States; nor shall any state deprive any person of life, liberty, or property, without due process of law; nor deny to any person within its jurisdiction the equal protection of the laws." The use of contraception came to be deemed one of these liberties, routinely designated "fundamental liberties," of which persons could not be deprived.

12. Justice Douglas, dissenting, in *Griswold*'s precursor *Poe v. Ullman*, 367 U.S. 497 (1961), had spoken of the "sanctity of the home" and of the bedroom as "the innermost sanctum of the home."

13. *Griswold v. Connecticut*.

14. *Bowers v. Hardwick*, 478 U.S. 186 (1986). A holding of the Court was "the fact that homosexual conduct occurs in the privacy of the home does not affect the result." Gerard Bradley, "Remaking the

Constitution: A Critical Reexamination of the *Bowers v. Hardwick* Dissent," *Wake Forest Law Review* 25 (1990): 501–546. Bradley argues that Hardwick "probably halted further development of the entire 'privacy' corpus" (504).

15. *Lawrence v. Texas.*

16. *Griswold v. Connecticut.*

17. *Eisenstadt v. Baird,* 405 U.S. 438 (1972), emphasis added.

18. In "Life's Dominion," Bradley has some interesting observations on the inclusion of the word "bear" in this formulation; he notes that *Eisenstadt* was argued before *Roe*, but decided after *Roe* (358). He calls *Eisenstadt* a "dress rehearsal for Roe" (359).

19. Bradley argues that contraception was not considered a fundamental right until *Roe*. "Life's Dominion," 359.

20. Douglas, opinion in *Griswold.*

21. *Griswold v. Connecticut.*

22. Ibid.

23. Ibid.

24. Ibid.

CHAPTER V
Roe *and Abortion*

1. *Roe v. Wade*, 410 U.S. 113 (1973).

2. An online review of pre-*Roe* abortion legislation can be found at James S. Cole, "Abortion Law before *Roe v. Wade*," http://www.missourilife.org/law/preroe.htm. Charges that the Court in *Roe* was guilty of judicial legislation have been frequent. An early classic article is Ely, "The Wages of Crying Wolf." See also Hittinger, "Abortion Before *Roe*," and Richard John Neuhaus, *The End of Democracy? The Judicial Usurpation of*

Politics—The Celebrated First Things *Debate with Arguments Pro and Con* (Dallas, TX: Spence, 1997).

3. Garrow details the history of the pro-abortion movement in *Liberty and Sexuality*, 37.

4. Lionel Tiger states, "It is impossible to overestimate the impact of the contraceptive pill on human arrangements. The most striking display of this is the baffling historical fact that after the pill became available in the mid-1960s, the pressure for liberal abortion intensified worldwide. This is remarkably, even profoundly, counterintuitive. It is also an implacable historical reality. Only after women could control their reproduction excellently did they need more and more safe abortions." *Decline of Males*, 35. See, for example, Henry P. David, ed., *From Abortion to Contraception: A Resource to Public Policies and Reproductive Behavior in Central and Eastern Europe from 1917 to the Present* (Westport, CT: Greenwood Press, 1999).

5. Robert T. Michael, "Why Did the U.S. Divorce Rate Double within a Decade?" *Research in Population Economics* 6 (Greenwich, CT: JAI Press, 1988), 361–399. See also his "Determinants of Divorce," in *Sociological Economics*, ed. Louis Levy-Garboua (London: Sage Publications, 1979), 223–254, and "The Rise in Divorce Rates, 1960–1974: Age-Specific Components," *Demography* 15.2 (May 1978): 177–182.

6. *Roe v. Wade*, emphasis added.

7. Ibid., emphasis added.

8. Ibid., emphasis added.

9. These pictures are available online at http://www.popphoto.com/americanphotofeatures/3497/life-by-lennart-nilsson.html.

10. *Roe v. Wade.*

11. The nineteenth-century movement against abortion was physician led. In 1859, the American

Medical Association gave several reasons for advocating laws against abortion, among them the view that human life begins before quickening. James S. Cole, "Abortion Law before *Roe v. Wade*," citing *Transactions of the American Medical Association* 13.12 (1859): 75–78.

12. O'Connor, dissenting in *Akron v. Akron Center for Reproductive Health*, 462 U.S. 416 (1983).

13. Naomi Wolf, "Our Bodies, Our Souls," *New Republic* (October 6, 1995), http://www.priestsforlife.org/prochoice/ourbodiesoursouls.htm.

14. Rehnquist in his dissent noted that "a transaction resulting in an operation such as this is not 'private' in the ordinary usage of that word." *Roe v. Wade*.

15. Ibid.

16. Ibid.

17. 505 U.S. 833 (1992).

18. Ibid.

19. See Erin Daly, "Reconsidering Abortion Law," on the significance of the change in terminology. She argues that appeal to "liberty" places the right to abortion on a firmer foundation.

20. *Planned Parenthood v. Casey*, emphasis added.

21. Ibid.

22. Ibid.

23. Ibid.

CHAPTER VI
Assisted Suicide and Homosexuality

1. Indeed, one churchman, Cardinal Cahal Daly some three decades ago predicted that contraception would lead to abortion and euthanasia, in *Morals, Law and Life* (Chicago: Scepter, 1996), 94–95, as cited

in Rice, *The Winning Side*, 2. See Rice, 112 to end, for further reflection on the connections. See also *Evangelium vitae*, nn. 13 and 15.

2. *Compassion in Dying v. Washington.*

3. *Vacco v. Quill*, 521 U.S. 793 (1997); *Washington v. Glucksberg*, 521 U.S. 792 (1997).

4. For the view that *Roe* would not have been possible had the Court been as honest in its judicial review of the prior legal status of abortion as it was in *Vacco* and *Glucksberg*, see Richard S. Myers, "Physician-Assisted Suicide," *National Catholic Bioethics Quarterly* 1.3 (Autumn 2001): 345–361. In "An Analysis of the Constitutionality of Laws Banning Assisted Suicide from the Perspective of Catholic Moral Teaching," Myers was prescient in his view that end-of-life cases were not employing the same method for determining reproductive issues. *University of Detroit Mercy Law Review* 72.4 (1995): 771–786,

5. References can be found in Appleton, "Assisted Suicide and Reproductive Freedom," footnote 1.

6. Appleton, "Assisted Suicide and Reproductive Freedom."

7. For example, *Quinlan* cites *Griswold* and *Roe*; *Casey* cites *Quinlan* and *Cruzan*; *Compassion in Dying* cites *Griswold*, *Roe*, and *Casey*. Oddly, *Vacco v. Quill* cites none of the privacy cases, but *Washington v. Glucksberg* has a significant discussion of liberty interests that include contraception and abortion. Indeed, *Washington v. Glucksberg* cites *Casey* against overextending the reach of personal autonomy.

8. *In re Quinlan*, 70 NJ 10, 355 A.2d 647 (NJ Supreme Court, 1976), http://philosophy.wisc.edu/streiffer/BioandLawF99Folder/Readings/In_re_Quinlan.pdf.

9. Ibid.

10. Ibid.

11. Ibid.

12. *Compassion in Dying v. Washington*.

13. For a good critique of the impossibility of rationally limiting the right to die, see Thomas J. Marzen, "'Out, Out Brief Candle': Constitutionally Prescribed Suicide for the Terminally Ill," *Hastings Constitutional Law Quarterly* 21 (Spring 1994): 799–826.

14. *Compassion in Dying v. Washington*.

15. In fact, *Glucksberg* rejected the historical analysis of *Compassion in Dying*. For comment on differences between *Glucksberg*'s treatment of the historical record and *Roe*'s, see Myers, "Physician-Assisted Suicide."

16. *Cruzan v. Director, MDH*, 497 U.S. 261 (1990).

17. See Wesley J. Smith, *Forced Exit: The Slippery Slope from Assisted Suicide to Legalized Murder* (New York: Random House, 1997), and, more recently, *Culture of Death: The Assault on Medical Ethics in America* (San Francisco: Encounter Books, 2000).

18. *Bowers v. Hardwick*, 478 U.S. 186 (1986). For a good analysis of the right to privacy and Bowers, see Bruce C. Hafen, "Individual Autonomy and Privacy: Are There Limits?" *Trust the Truth: A Symposium on the Twentieth Anniversary of the Encyclical* Humanae vitae, ed. Russell E. Smith (Braintree, MA: Pope John Center), 103–123.

19. *Lawrence v. Texas*.

20. Edward Stein, "Introducing *Lawrence v. Texas*: Some Background and a Glimpse of the Future," *Cardozo Women's Law Journal* 10 (Winter 2004): 263–288.

21. *Lawrence v. Texas*, emphasis added.

22. *Goodridge v. Department of Public Health*, 798 N.E.2d 941 (Mass. 2003).

Notes

Chapter VII
Political Connections and Natural Consequences

1. John T. McGreevy, *Catholicism and American Freedom* (New York: W. W. Norton, 2003), 226.

2. Gene Burns, *The Moral Veto: Framing Contraception, Abortion, and Cultural Pluralism in the United States* (Cambridge, U.K.: Cambridge University Press, 2005).

3. Angela Franks, *Margaret Sanger's Eugenic Legacy: The Control of Female Fertility* (Jefferson, NC: McFarland, 2005).

4. See Planned Parenthood Web site, http://www.plannedparenthood.org.

5. *Buck v. Bell*, 274 U.S. 200 (1927).

6. See, for example, "Planned Parenthood," Life Education and Resource Network Northeast Web site, http://blackgenocide.org/planned.html.

7. See Donald T. Critchlow, *Intended Consequences, Birth Control, and the Federal Government in Modern America* (New York: Oxford University Press, 1999).

8. See McGreevy, *Catholicism and American Freedom*, ch. 8, and Michael Warner, *Changing Witness: Catholic Bishops and Public Policy 1917–1994* (Grand Rapids, MI: Wm. B. Eerdmans, 1995).

9. Tentler, *Catholics and Contraception*, 53.

10. Ibid., 56.

11. McGreevy, *Catholicism and American Freedom*, 223.

12. Ibid., 231.

13. Tentler, *Catholics and Contraception*, 162–172.

14. See Critchlow, *Intended Consequences*, 118–128.

15. John T. McGreevy, "John Courtney Murray, Contraception, and the 'Liberal Catholic' Justification for Abortion," The Church and the Liberal Tradition Web site, http://www.ratzingerfanclub.com/liberalism/murray_contraception_abortion.html.

16. "The Connecticut statute confuses the moral and legal, in that it transposes without further ado a private sin into a public crime. The criminal act here is the private use of contraceptives. The real area where the coercions of law might, and ought to, be applied, at least to control an evil—namely, the contraceptive industry—is quite overlooked. As it stands, the statute is, of course, unenforceable without police invasion of the bedroom, and is therefore indefensible as a piece of legal draughtsmanship." John Courtney Murray, *We Hold These Truths: Catholic Reflections on the American Proposition* (New York: Sheed & Ward, 1960), 157–158.

17. Critchlow, *Intended Consequences*, 63–65.

18. McGreevy, "John Courtney Murray."

19. Warner, *Changing Witness*, 106.

20. On November 14, 2006, the U.S. Conference of Catholic Bishops issued "Married Love and the Gift of Life," which defends the Church's teaching on contraception (http://www.usccb.org/laity/marriage/MarriedLove.pdf). In recent years several bishops have issued statements of support for *Humanae vitae*. One of the first was by Archbishop Charles Chaput, O.F.M. Cap., "Of Human Life," July 22, 1998 (http://www.archden.org/archbishop_writings_discourses/pastoral_letter/pl_Jul22_98_OfHumanLife.pdf).

21. Tentler, *Catholics and Contraception*.

22. For a report on this event, see NCCB Secretariat for Pro-Life Activities, "A Chronicle of Euthanasia Trends in America," *Life at Risk* 8.8 (November 1998), http://www.usccb.org/prolife/publicat/liferisk/nov98.shtml

23. See U.S. Conference of Catholic Bishops, "Bishop sees growing support for a marriage protection amendment," press release, May 25, 2006, http://www.usccb.org/comm/archives/2006/06-105.shtml. The statement was by Bishop Joseph E. Kurtz, of Knoxville, Tennessee, Chairman of the Committee on Marriage and Family for the USCCB.

24. Archdiocese of Boston, "Statement by Archbishop Seán O'Malley on Catholic Charities decision to withdraw from adoption services," press release, March 10, 2006, http://www.rcab.org/News/releases/2006/statement060310.html.

25. William Breitbart and Barry D. Rosenfeld, "Physician-Assisted Suicide: The Influence of Psychosocial Issues," *Cancer Control* 6.2 (March/April 1999):146–161, http://www.moffitt.org/moffittapps/ccj/v6n2/article3.htm.

26. *Planned Parenthood v. Casey*.

27. Rice, *Winning Side*, 87.

28. The organization NARTH (National Association for Research and Therapy of Homosexuality), www.narth.org, has an abundance of good sources for understanding homosexuality.

29. The work of Patrick Fagan at the Heritage Foundation, www.heritage.org, provides excellent documentation of these connections.